66

S0-BHX-117

K.3.3

THE FORGIVENESS OF SINS

A COURSE OF SERMONS

By the same Author

CHRIST'S TEMPTATION AND OURS. The Baldwin Lectures, 1896.

THE USE OF HOLY SCRIPTURE IN THE WORSHIP OF THE CHURCH. The Paddock Lectures, 1903.

THE CHRISTIAN DOCTRINE OF PRAYER. The Bohlen Lectures, 1904.

THE RELATIONS OF FAITH AND LIFE. The Bedell Lectures, 1905.

THE EXAMPLE OF OUR LORD.

CONFIRMATION. In the Oxford Library of Practical Theology.

THE VIRGIN MOTHER. Addresses on the Life of the Blessed Virgin Mary as told in the Gospels. With an Appended Essay on the Virgin Birth of our Lord Jesus Christ.

THE CHURCH'S DISCIPLINE CONCERNING MARRIAGE AND DIVORCE. A charge. 1896.

MARRIAGE WITH RELATIVES. A charge. 1901.

ECCLESIASTICAL DISCIPLINE. A charge. 1904.

THE EUCHARIST. A charge. 1907.

THE

FORGIVENESS OF SINS

A COURSE OF SERMONS

BY

THE RT. REV. A. C. A. HALL, D.D., LL.D.

BISHOP OF VERMONT

LONGMANS, GREEN, AND CO.
91 AND 93 FIFTH AVENUE, NEW YORK
LONDON AND BOMBAY
1908

Copyright, 1908

By Longmans, Green, and Co.

NOTE

THESE sermons were preached in St. Paul's Church, Burlington, and in St. Stephen's, Middlebury, during Lent, 1907. They have since been written out, with some notes, in the hope that they may be more widely helpful, as putting into harmonious relation several matters of belief and practice which are apt to be thought of disjointedly. The seventh sermon was preached later at the ordination of a priest, and is added as bearing on the same general subject.

CONTENTS

I

THE NATURE AND POSSIBILITY OF FORGIVENESS

I

THE NATURE AND POSSIBILITY OF FORGIVENESS

Have mercy upon me, O God, after thy great goodness:
according to the multitude of thy mercies do away mine offences.
Wash me throughly from my wickedness:
and cleanse me from my sin.   *Psalm* li. 1, 2.

I. THE Forgiveness of Sins is an article of the
Creed. It has its place in the short summary of
great truths in which we profess as Christians to
believe. First of all I would beg you to dwell upon
the significance of this fact. We do not express our
belief in what is obvious; the things we believe are
truths which God has made known to us, that men
did not and could not find out for themselves. We
do not declare our belief in our own existence here
and now: this is a matter of sensible experience.
We believe in the existence of God, unseen and
purely spiritual in His being, acting and working
behind and through laws and instrumentalities and
agencies, the Maker and Ruler of all things in heaven
and earth, visible and invisible. We believe in the
continued existence of our personal being, with powers
of thought and affection and choice, after the disso-
lution of this material envelope of our physical organ-

3

ization, after the crash and shock of death. We believe further in the resurrection of the body, the restoration of the whole of our complex nature, physical and spiritual, to its integrity, in however changed a condition.[1] There is a certain difficulty about all the things which we believe, however truly reasonable they may be when explained. We believe in God, the Father, the Son, and the Holy Ghost, our Creator, Redeemer, and Sanctifier; we believe in the Holy Catholic Church, the Resurrection of the body, and the Life everlasting; we believe also in the Forgiveness of Sins. It is not plain and obvious.

II. Now this consideration does not at all fit in, you will recognize, with the way in which a great many people speak and think about the Forgiveness of Sins. This they regard as the most obvious thing in the world; it is to their mind perfectly natural and easy, something to be taken for granted rather than treated as a subject of Christian revelation and belief. On the one hand, *God*, they say, is not injured by man's sin. It cannot hurt Him. So there is nothing much to forgive. And anyhow He is good and easy, not exacting; He will not take offence. He will let off everybody. All will come right at last.[2] And on

---

[1] Phil. iii. 20, 21.

[2] On the necessary wrath of a Holy Being against that which is contrary to His will and nature, see Du Bose, *The Gospel according*

the other hand, *man* is frail. His faults must not be taken too seriously. He has a corrupt and disordered nature; or, if that be considered an old-fashioned idea, all will agree that he is easily tempted; his higher faculties of reason and conscience swayed and overborne by his passions, appetites, and fancies. Some would even argue that the Christian Church makes a mistake in speaking of sin as something which needs Forgiveness. What we call moral evil may after all only be a step, in many cases a necessary step, upward to goodness. We must have some experience of evil before we can choose goodness, so they argue. Perhaps reason and conscience have not as yet asserted themselves. This part of human nature is undeveloped. Man is still in the merely animal stage. Men trip and stumble in morals, as a child in learning to walk, as an apprentice makes

to St. Paul, ch. v., "The Wrath of God against sin." "If, as Bishop Butler says, all experience of life shows what part God takes in it, on what side He is, viz. on the side of righteousness and against unrighteousness; if the agnosticism of Matthew Arnold can see clearly enough that the power not ourselves in the affairs of men makes for righteousness only and wholly, it was not too much for the more spiritual vision of St. Paul to discern that to say that the Righteous Lord loveth righteousness can mean no more nor less than that He hates unrighteousness. [Rom. i. 18.] And indeed no terms can express too strongly the wrath of God actually revealed in nature and in human affairs against the ungodliness and unrighteousness of men as it exists in the world. St. Paul expresses himself neither otherwise than as the actual facts revealed, nor more strongly than the actual facts justified." P. 60.

blunders in learning a trade, or a student in acquiring a language.

III. Now against any such light view of sin as this, however plausibly it may be urged, a healthy conscience protests as fallacious. For look you! No pricks of conscience, no sense of remorse, follow upon the one kind of failure,—for instance, to keep upright when we are trying to skate, or to conjugate a verb correctly, or to find a place upon the map,—save of course when the failure shows carelessness or neglect in preparing a lesson. But if a man commits a moral fault, — tells a lie, loses his temper, and gives vent to unkind speech, or yields to sensual indulgence,—then there is a distinct sense of shame, a " self-contempt bitterer than blood," as Shelley says.[1] Such a fault is followed by a feeling of uneasiness, a desire to disguise the fact and hide it from others, sometimes by a reluctance to acknowledge it even to ourselves, Though the conscience may be for a while drugged and dulled, it is ready to spring up at some crisis in our experience; in a serious illness it gives an added horror to the approach of death.

We recognize sin to be something more than a mistake in the sphere of morals. A mistake indeed it is, egregious folly, missing the true end of our life,[2]

[1] *Prometheus unbound*, Act II, scene iv.

[2] This is the literal meaning of ἁμαρτία, the common word in

supposing that to be valuable which is really worthless or hurtful; but it is a mistake for which we are,
in part at least, responsible. It is the rejection of a
higher law of which we are conscious. In spite of
manifold excuses we have to acknowledge that there
has been a wilful transgression of what we knew to
be right. We have done that which we *ought* not to
have done; we have left undone that which we *ought*
to have done. It is by our own great fault that we
have sinned.

IV. It is well worth while to note that there is a
great deal in modern thought to confirm these protests of conscience, a great deal that is utterly op-
posed to the popular and easy regard of sin. Note
two points: (a) We are learning to recognize in-
creasingly the reign of law. Things are as they are,
not by chance, but as the expression of unfailing
laws. This applies to the sphere of morals as well
as to the material universe. God's commandments
are not arbitrarily laid down. Take, for instance,
the Sixth, Seventh, and Eighth of the Ten Commandments. Hatred and injury of others, adultery and
uncleanness, dishonesty and untruthfulness, are not
whimsically prohibited; they could not have been

the New Testament for sin. See Trench, *Synonyms of the New
Testament*, LXVI. This is the idea expressed by the use of
"Folly" for moral wrong in the Wisdom literature.

right. In the very nature of things, truth and purity, love and respect for others, belong to the constitution of human society, however God may for a time have tolerated a lower than the highest fulfilment of these principles. Sin, then, the transgression of these commandments, is not a mere personal affront to God; it introduces into human life and conduct an element of moral disorder. It breaks a law of the universe. And every breach of the moral law brings its inevitable consequence, its punishment, if you like to call it so,[1] just as does a violation of the laws of physical health. You drink impure water, and you run the risk, at any rate, of typhoid fever; you breathe tainted air, and you may get consumption; you eat unwholesome or insufficient food, or neglect proper exercise, and your physical health and strength is impaired. Nature, mark you, knows no forgiveness. With her there is no return of opportunity, no obliteration of the past. The deed done remains while the world lasts. The deed left undone is a blank forever. Sin in every form is a violation of law, and law inexorably requires its penalty to the utmost.[2] There is a moral order in the universe which

[1] God executes the law; but His wrath is ordinarily manifested through natural causes and consequences in the actual working of things. Du Bose, *Gospel according to St. Paul*, p. 60.

[2] Westcott, *Historic Faith*, p. 130; *Gospel of the Resurrection*, p. 167; comp. Aubrey Moore, *From Advent to Advent*, sermon xviii, "The Forgiveness of Sins."

links together sin and doom. Retribution is the law of the universe, material and moral, that obtains here and hereafter. To reason the great mystery of the future is not punishment, but forgiveness. (b) For remember further, moral offences have not only an external but also an internal effect. It is not only that God is insulted, or that our neighbor in one way or another is wronged; sin also affects ourselves. There is the law of habit as well as the law of retribution. "Whatsoever a man soweth, that shall he also reap." [1] We sow our thoughts, and we reap our actions; we sow our actions, and we reap our habits; we sow our habits, and we reap our characters; we sow our characters, and we reap our destiny.

It becomes easier to do wrong. Our conscience is dulled and grows less sensitive; our will is weakened and less able to resist the pressure of pleasure or of pain; our affections are perverted. Then arises the question, How can this downward tendency be arrested? How can man's moral nature be restored, his equilibrium be recovered? This is evidently a matter of difficulty; the Forgiveness of Sins is not the simple matter we had imagined.

There are those who would say, Any restoration is impossible. Your attempts at the reformation of the outcast or the drunkard or the thief are idle; it

[1] Gal. vi. 7, 8; comp. Rev. xxii. 11, 12.

is kind of you to desire to undertake such a task, but it is really a waste of time and labor and money. Heredity, environment, and habit are too strong. You are doomed to disappointment.

V. Here comes in the Christian Religion, declaring that these things are possible, however difficult. These are its glad tidings, that evil habits can be overcome, that man can be restored, put at peace with himself and with God, his equilibrium regained, his nature reconstituted after the image of Him who created him, in righteousness and true holiness.[1] This is the Gospel assurance, — God so loved the world of mankind (even in their fallen condition), that He gave His only begotten Son, that whosoever believeth in Him (not by a mere trust in what He has done, but by a real surrender of self to Him) should not perish (in a withered, worthless existence), but should have eternal life.[2] This was the "faithful saying," repeated among the early disciples, "Christ Jesus came into the world to save sinners" — not to save them while sinners from the consequence of their sins, but to save them from their sins.[3] He came with an offer of help, with the assurance of the possibility of forgiveness, that the diverted stream

---

[1] Eph. iv. 24, Col. iii. 10.
[2] John iii. 16.
[3] 1 Tim. i. 15; comp. Matt. i. 21.

of human life might be turned back into its proper course.

And the Christian Church points to instances of men and women, individuals and communities, in whose experience this promise has been realized. Listen to St. Paul writing to the Corinthians. He has spoken of different classes of open and outrageous sins in which they had lived in their heathen state, before acknowledging Jesus Christ as Lord and Master. Neither sensualists nor drunkards nor covetous nor revilers — none such, he says, shall inherit the kingdom of God. And then he goes on: "And such were some of you: but ye washed yourselves, ye were consecrated, ye were justified in the name of the Lord Jesus, and by the Spirit of our God." [1]

The Forgiveness of Sins, then, though difficult, has been made possible. Its nature and meaning we are to trace; in particular the *condition* required on our part to gain it, repentance; the *grounds* which make it possible on God's part, the work of our Lord Jesus Christ; the *means* by which the gift is brought home and applied to us personally, one by one, the sacraments of the Church.

VI. From what has been said you will recognize that (1) while Forgiveness is not the easy thing that

---

[1] 1 Cor. vi. 9–11, ἀπελούσασθε, ἡγιάσθητε, ἐδικαιώθητε.

popular religion often represents it, (2) it is at the same time something far grander, much more worthy of God to bestow, of man to seek. Forgiveness contains two elements. It is no mere letting off of punishment, or remitting of debt. It is restoration as well as acquittal.[1] God does not desire to surround Himself with a crowd of forgiven criminals; He would transform them into a family of adopted children. In His acceptance of the penitent sinner God's mercy plays no trick upon His justice. There is no regarding as righteous one who is really clothed in filthy rags, because the robe of Christ's righteousness is thrown over him, as if God's eye would not see through the fiction. There is nothing unreal about justification; it is no merely forensic or legal process. God declares men righteous because He makes them righteous. He counts indeed the initial surrender of ourselves to Him as containing in itself the germ of all the development that shall follow. He takes men as they are, that He may gradually make them what they should be. "Cleanse me from sin's guilt and power" is the penitent's prayer.

This twofold character should belong, in some degree at any rate, to all Forgiveness. We must not

---

[1] 1 John i. 9. This is the force of ἀφίημι and of *Remissio*. "Apart from questions of etymology and derivation God's Forgiveness does contain, and in the N. T. is represented as containing, far more than acquittal." — Du Bose, *Gospel according to St. Paul*, pp. 116, 76, 285.

be content with remitting a penalty; we must seek
the restoration of the offender. All discipline and
punishment ought to have in view this object.

(a) Let me apply it for a moment to our civil
institutions. We have our county jails and our
state prisons. We are bound to use any influence
we have to make them really houses of correction.
A man or woman is put in prison not merely that a
penalty may be exacted, not merely to express the
frown of the community upon the wrong-doing; the
object and endeavor ought further to be that, when
he has served his sentence and paid his penalty, the
discharged prisoner may go forth not hardened in
crime, not more degraded by reason of association
with criminals worse than himself, but prepared to
be a respectable and useful member of the community. For this he should be fitted not only by having
learned an honest trade, but also by having been
taught what is far more important, moral principles.
How far are our reformatory institutions realizing
this aim? The old days of branding criminals with
a mark of their crime on clothes or flesh, so that they
could not lift up their heads or hope to get respectable employment, are gone. But are we careful not
to condemn to recklessness those whom it is our duty
to try by all means to reform and restore?

(b) In the spiritual sphere the Church is such a
reformatory home, a spiritual infirmary for sin-sick

souls, where they are to be nursed back to health and strength. There must, of course, be a willingness, as with a patient in a hospital, to accept rule and regimen, to take a nauseous medicine, to submit if necessary to the surgeon's knife. What seems like severe treatment may be the veriest kindness. Restoration to life is the object of all. This is possible, but it is difficult. It required the Passion of our Lord Jesus Christ. It demands something corresponding with this on our part to claim and appropriate our share in its benefits. It requires direct intervention on God's part, and careful effort on ours.

You see the possibility and the nature of Forgiveness. "If we confess our sins, God is faithful and just to forgive us our sins, and to cleanse us from all unrighteousness." [1] That is God's promise. And this shall be our prayer:

"Have mercy upon me, O God, after thy great goodness: according to the multitude of thy mercies do away mine offences.
Wash me throughly from my wickedness:
and cleanse me from my sin."

[1] 1 John i. 9.

II

REPENTANCE THE CONDITION OF FORGIVENESS

II

REPENTANCE THE CONDITION OF FORGIVENESS

I know the thoughts that I think toward you, saith the LORD, thoughts of peace, and not of evil, to give you hope in your latter end. Then shall ye call upon me, and ye shall go and pray unto me, and I will hearken unto you. And ye shall seek me, and find me, when ye shall search for me with all your heart.

Jeremiah xxix. 11–13.

Now I rejoice, not that ye were made sorry, but that ye sorrowed to repentance: for ye were made sorry after a godly manner, that ye might receive damage by us in nothing. For godly sorrow worketh repentance to salvation which bringeth no regret: but the sorrow of the world worketh death. For behold this selfsame thing, that ye sorrowed after a godly sort, what carefulness it wrought in you, yea, what clearing of yourselves, yea, what indignation, yea, what fear, yea, what vehement desire, yea, what zeal, yea, what revenge! In all things ye have approved yourselves to be clear in this matter.

2 Corinthians vii. 9–11.

I. THE Forgiveness of Sins we have seen to be something far less easy and obvious than people are apt to suppose. Nature knows no forgiveness. A transgression or breach of the order of the universe, material or moral, brings its inevitable consequences. Sin and doom are firmly riveted together. Whatever we sow, that we must reap. Forgiveness involves a direct intervention of Almighty God to counteract the consequence, to avert the doom.

At the same time we have seen Forgiveness to be a far grander thing than the popular conception of it, since it means not only acquittal but also restoration: not so much the remission of the penalty as the restoration of the offender.

II. We are to think now of the condition required on our part for obtaining God's forgiveness. The condition is Repentance. What is comprised in Repentance, its several elements, we must examine; but first in general we recognize that there must be on our part a genuine desire to be forgiven.

Forgiveness means reconciliation. And reconciliation must be mutual; it cannot be one-sided. Though the advance may be made by one party, both parties must concur. A hand is extended; it must be grasped. The barriers on either side must be thrown down. This is the case with reconciliation and forgiveness amongst ourselves. You will remember our Lord's words, "If thy brother sin against thee, rebuke him; and if he repent, forgive him; and if he sin against thee seven times in the day, and seven times turn again to thee, saying I repent, thou shalt forgive him." [1] That, of course, is not to be understood literally, but as enjoining unlimited forgiveness on the

---

[1] Luke xvii. 3, 4. The meaning of the first clause is clearly "sin (or trespass) *against thee*," though the words ἐπί σε are not found in the best readings.

condition of genuine repentance. We cannot forgive, we are not bidden or expected to do so, without repentance, and its expression in some kind of apology, nor in the face of continued and persistent hostility on the part of another. We must be in a readiness to forgive; we must not cherish a sense of wrong; we must not impose what are practically impossible conditions; we must make some advance, meet the other person, as we say, half way; we may try to win him by showing kindnesses: but with all our good intentions, if the other person prove obdurate, we may be baffled and repelled. There must be a desire on his part to be reconciled.

And forgiveness means more than reconciliation; it includes, so far as possible, restoration to the old position. If we recur to the illustration of the hospital which I used before, the doctor and nurse are not content to send out a patient permanently maimed or incapable. They aim at restored health and vigor. Even after an amputation they may provide an artificial limb. But there will often be a lengthened season of convalescence. Perfect physical health and strength are not regained at once. So it is with the restoration of a friendship; this may take time in proportion to the gravity of the wrong, the character and nature of the alienation; where, for instance, there has been a betrayal of confidence, the person must prove himself again trustworthy before we can impart to him our secrets. And so it is with our moral restoration. Knots have to be untied, tangles straightened out; we cannot all at once spring back to the position we have forfeited by our sins. There may be necessary a long spiritual convalescence, even a lifetime of penitence. But — this is what I want to impress upon you — God's aim and desire is to bring us back to a condition of holiness, of real rightness and integrity of life. To this He called us at our Baptism. We are in the end to get to the same place, though it may be by a longer and rougher path. Holiness is to be regained through penitence, if not preserved in innocence.

III. Moreover, this restoration, we must remember, may become impossible, through the loss of the genuine desire for forgiveness. Repentance may become impossible. This is the dreadful warning given in the Epistle to the Hebrews: "It is impossible for those who were once enlightened, and tasted of the heavenly gift, and were made partakers of the Holy Spirit, and tasted the good word of God and the powers of the world to come, and after this fell away, it is impossible again to renew them unto repentance." [1] Mark you, it is not that any sin, however

[1] Hebrews vi. 4–6; comp. x. 26–29. The writer is dealing primarily with apostasy. So far as our sin approaches this, the consequence becomes the same. Apostasy may be practical, in life, as well as theoretical, in unbelief.

grievous, is beyond God's power to forgive, if only
the sinner truly repents. But it is this which becomes
more and more difficult. Such persons as the writer
contemplates have used up their privileges, have
sinned against light, have done despite to the Spirit
of grace. Habits become fixed, and character formed,
the desire for good fades away; a man has called
evil good so long that it becomes *his* good; the conscience is dulled, the affections are perverted, the
will is weakened. Sin may become unpardonable
because the person has lost the power of repentance.
This, which is in accordance with much that we may
experience in ourselves and observe in the world
around us, is the explanation of the New Testament
warnings as to the possibility of future and unending
loss. It is not that God inflicts everlasting punishment for temporary sins: it is rather that, in spite
of all His loving purpose for us, men may bring upon
themselves unending and irremediable wreck and
ruin.[1] An earthly father may be disappointed in his
fondest hopes, and thwarted in his most cherished
plans for his son, by the son's perversity. The boy
by his folly or negligence may render himself abso-

---

[1] Mark iii. 29, ἔνοχός ἐστιν αἰωνίου ἁμαρτήματος. "The man
is in the grasp of his sin, which will not let him go without a Divine
ἄφεσις, and to this sin the power exercised by the Son of man
does not apply, since it is αἰώνιον." — H. B. Swete *in loc.* See a
sermon, "Sin and Penalty," by the late R. W. Church, in *Human
Life and its conditions.*

lutely unfitted for the place which his father intended for him, for which he sought to prepare and train him.

It is not — this it is important to keep clear — that the person has no perception of the misery and loss which he has incurred, or of the loss and degradation to which he has sunk by his own fault,— this may at times be very acute,— but the trouble is that he has not will and energy enough to rise up and battle with the causes which have brought about these consequences.

IV. Here we see the meaning of the distinction made by St. Paul between what he calls a godly sorrow that leads to repentance and salvation, and the sorrow of the world which worketh death. By the sorrow of the world he means a sorrow for sin and wrong-doing that springs only or chiefly from its temporal consequences,— the loss, it may be, of means or health, of position or character, the shame in which others too are involved. This sorrow, the apostle says, works death. We are perfectly familiar with what St. Paul thus describes. You may see illustrations of it in almost every newspaper that you open. Here is a poor girl who has been betrayed and has lost her character. She cannot bear the consequences, she cannot face the parents on whom she has brought disgrace. She throws herself over a bridge, or takes poison. There is a clerk in an office or store, who has been speculating with money which did not belong to him, and has lost heavily. The day of reckoning and exposure is at hand. He cannot stand it. He buys a revolver and blows out his brains. See the sorrow of the world that worketh death! Or in less literal forms than these it not less truly works death. A student has wasted his time and opportunities, has got into bad ways. He goes railroading or mining, or is found loafing about a race-track or the billiard-room of a hotel. He has thrown up everything. What's the good? he says. It might have been worth while once, but now there is no hope. His recklessness is a form of death.

Contrasted with this is what the apostle calls a godly sorrow that brings about repentance leading on to salvation, to moral rescue, and a condition of restored spiritual health: a repentance, this, that brings no regret. Godly sorrow is that which takes God into account, which recognizes sin, whatever its other consequences, as an offence against a righteous Ruler, a generous Benefactor, a loving Father.[1] And

---

[1] Ps. li. 4, "Against thee, thee only, have I sinned." The other aspects of his deed — its heinous criminality as a wrong done to a fellow-man — disappeared for the time, while he contemplated it as a sin against his infinitely gracious Benefactor."
—W. Kay.

so, while overwhelmed with shame and grief, there is
no deadening remorse or recklessness. The recogni-
tion of God's goodness, which deepens the sense of
wrong, makes the penitent to be not without hope.
Although offended, a Father still.[1] He takes up the
cry of the prodigal son, I will return to my father;
though unworthy to be called his son, I will surrender myself to him in penitence and trust; let him
treat me as he will.[2]

V. We see at once that this godly sorrow includes
a great deal more than is ordinarily thought of under
the name of Repentance. The word in the Greek
Testament which we translate Repentance, and
which stands for the condition of Forgiveness, which
leads to salvation, is something far more than a
feeling of compunction, or a mere mourning and
lamenting over offences. Quite literally it means a
change of mind, not in the vulgar sense of fickleness,

[1] Bp. Andrewes, "Sermons on the Lord's Prayer," VII: "The
master may cease to be a master, so may a servant; the husband
may cease to be a husband, so may the wife by means of divorce;
but God can never cease to be 'our Father' though He be never
so much offended, and we cannot cease to be His sons how wicked
soever we be; and therefore God doth by an immutable term
signify unto us the immutability of His affection."

[2] Luke xv. 18, 19. "The well-spring of repentance is *faith*,
first breeding *fear*, and then *love*; which love causeth *hope*, hope
resolution of attempt, — 'I will go to my Father.'" — Hooker,
Eccl. Pol., VI. iii. 4.

but as a deliberate change of *purpose* based on a change of *view*.[1] It is first intellectual, not sentimental, or at any rate the intellectual perceptions and faculties are first appealed to and affected in this change of mind. A wider horizon is gained; new considerations are taken in; a fresh point of view is obtained; true standards are recognized. Then follow, quite naturally, new and different emotional experiences, and these again create new desires and purposes. There is a change of mind — as regards the past, a real desire that the wrong had not been; as regards the future, a firm purpose that it shall not be again.

We may go through, in a practical way, the elements of this acceptable Repentance that leads to salvation.

1. There is the *mind* of Repentance. We "take upon ourselves a new mind." Whereas we had thought most of material things, spiritual considerations now gain the first place. Temporal interests are seen to be less important than those which are eternal. We had thought of ourselves, our pleasure, our advancement; these had been ruling considera-

---

[1] See Treadwell Walden's essay, *The great meaning of Metanoia*, and these explanations of the word by Bp. Westcott: "A complete change of mind, consequent upon the apprehension of the true moral nature of things"; " a complete change of the intellectual, moral, spiritual state." *Epistle to the Hebrews*, pp. 150, 147.

tions: now we are learning to ask not, How shall
I please myself? but, What is God's will? How
can I best glorify Him, and most truly serve my
brethren?

The mind of Repentance requires a knowledge of
sin, and this will be gained by self-examination, see-
ing where and what we are in comparison with the
true standards of God's commandments and our
baptismal obligations and privileges.[1]

2. The mind of Repentance will lead to the *heart*
of Repentance, not a change only from motives of
policy and prudence or fear, but a real sorrow for
what has offended God. On this we have already
dwelt.

3. And this will be expressed in the *word* of Repentance, as we acknowledge and confess our faults.
This, as the utterance of the mind and heart, sometimes stands for the whole of Repentance, as in St.
John's promise, "If we confess our sins, God is
faithful and just to forgive us our sins, and to cleanse
us from all unrighteousness." [2]   Remember, we are
to confess not our *sinfulness* — throwing the blame
perhaps upon God for having given us a frail nature,
for allowing us to be exposed to the pressure of hered-

[1] 1 Cor. xi. 28, 2 Cor. xiii. 5.

[2] 1 John i. 9. The word of confession or apology, of course, is
worthless unless it have behind it the heart's sorrow, and the
heart's feeling is valueless unless it be the child of conviction and
the parent of action.

ity or environment — but our *sins*, the things which we have done that we ought not to have done, the things we have left undone that we ought to have done; our sins of thought and word and deed, through pride and selfishness, through covetousness and worldliness, through sensuality and indulgence. We must call our sins by their true names; thus and thus have I sinned by my own great fault.[1]

4. The mind and heart of Repentance, expressed in words, will be carried out in *works* meet for Repentance, works that befit such a change of mind. These will be various;[2] some especially stand out clearly.

(a) The most obvious is amendment of life, reversing the former wrong choice. We shall say, "Yes, Lord, with Thy help I will shoulder this burden, face this duty, submit to this sacrifice or humiliation,"

---

[1] "To call ourselves sinners availeth nothing, except we lay our faults in the balance, and take the weight of them one by one." — Chrysostom, Hom. xxxi on Hebrews xii. 14, etc.

[2] "Amongst the works of satisfaction, the most respected have been always these three, Prayers, Fasts, and Alms-deeds: by prayer, we lift up our souls to him from whom sin and iniquity have withdrawn them; by fasting, we reduce the body from thraldom under vain delights, and make it serviceable for parts of virtuous conversation; by alms, we dedicate to charity those worldly goods and possessions, which unrighteousness doth neither get nor bestow well: the first, a token of piety intended towards God; the second, a pledge of moderation and sobriety in the carriage of our own persons; the last, a testimony of our meaning to do good to all men." — Hooker, *Eccl. Pol.*, VI. v. 6.

where before in cowardly fashion we hung back, saying, "No, I can't," or in rebellion, "No, I won't." We shall say now, "No, by God's help I will not yield to this indulgence or to this offer of unlawful gain," where before we said, "Yes, I must."

(b) Amendment of life will carry with it the careful avoiding in the future of temptations which past experience has shown to be dangerous for us. It may be some companionship which has proved lowering, or some reading which has stained our imagination or needlessly suggested doubts. You have seen a moth on a summer evening fly fascinated to the flame; its wings are singed; now, you say, it will keep away. No, it is drawn by a fatal attraction; it is scorched. Once again, and it is consumed. How often do men and women act in the same foolish fashion — singed, scorched, consumed by temptation! They delight to skate on thin ice, the very danger apparently proving attractive.[1]

(c) More than this. There will be, there must be, a serious endeavor to make reparation for injuries done to another's name or property or feelings, — much more for injury to his character which we may have lowered by our persuasion or example. Restitution, when possible, is a necessary element of true

[1] In severe contrast with such conduct is our Lord's warning, Matt. v. 29, 30: "His counsel is, Seek after purity of heart, and count no sacrifice too costly or too painful that you may win it." — David Smith, *The days of His flesh*, pp. 99, 100.

repentance, a condition of forgiveness. What we wish had been undone, we must so far as possible undo. You remember the story of Zacchæus, the man in public office who had grown rich through dishonest means.[1] When our Lord invited Himself to his house, Zacchæus felt he must shake himself free from his ill-gotten gains before he could receive such a guest. So, standing at the door of his house, he declares, Lord, if I have done wrong to any man, I here and now promise to restore him fourfold, which was more than the law required.[2] And because there were many whom he had defrauded that he could not reach, the remainder of his money he divided into two parts, and half he gave to the poor. At any cost he must get rid of what was not lawfully his.

(d) Close akin to restitution where we have wronged another is the duty of forgiving any who may have injured us. This is a work of repentance required by our Lord Himself. Unreadiness to forgive others is a token that we are not truly penitent before God, that we do not realize the greatness of our indebtedness to Him.[3]

(e) Once more: where there is true penitence there will be a desire to manifest and prove sorrow for having grieved and offended God. There will be a gladness at the opportunity to bear pain or give

[1] Luke xix. 1–10.   [2] Levit. vi. 5.   [3] Matthew xviii. 21–35.

up pleasure, to take shame, as a proof of our "loyal and loving change."

Thus we see the meaning of these manifestations of godly sorrow which St. Paul enumerates, whether we think of them as realized in the Corinthian Church collectively or in an individual Christian:

What *carefulness* it wrought in you, what a serious view you now take! carefulness will be shown in self-examination.

What *clearing of yourselves* from the wrong — in confession!

What *indignation* against the wrong!

What *fear*, when you think of the offence against God!

What *vehement desire and longing* for true reconciliation!

What *zeal* now to make progress in the right path!

What *revenge* in proving your loving sorrow!

Then shall be realized the gracious promise: " I know the thoughts that I think toward you, saith the Lord; thoughts of peace and not of evil, to give you hope in your latter end. Ye shall call upon me, and ye shall go and pray unto me, and I will hearken unto you, and ye shall seek me and find me, when ye shall seek me with all your hearts."

III

OUR LORD'S SACRIFICE THE GROUND OF FORGIVENESS

III

OUR LORD'S SACRIFICE THE GROUND OF FORGIVENESS

The God of our fathers raised up Jesus, whom ye slew and hanged on a tree. Him hath God exalted with his right hand to be a Prince and a Saviour, for to give repentance to Israel, and forgiveness of sins. — *Acts* v. 30, 31.

HE, mark you, Jesus Christ our Lord, gives both — Repentance and Remission or Forgiveness of sins. This is early apostolic teaching, in one of St. Peter's first recorded speeches. It is an echo of our Lord's own words at the end of St. Luke's Gospel. In the days of the Resurrection, we are told, He opened the mind of His disciples, that they might understand the Scriptures — the real meaning of the Old Testament — and He said unto them, Thus it is written — in all sorts of prophecies and figures — that the Christ — the promised Deliverer — should suffer, and rise again from the dead the third day, and that repentance and remission of sins should be proclaimed in His name unto all the nations.[1]

Repentance is man's part, not an idle compunction for the past, nor a mere improvement in external

[1] Luke xxiv. 45–47.

behavior for the future, leaving the past untouched; but an entire change of mind, the man turning now with mind and heart and will to God, from whom he was alienated.[1] Forgiveness is God's act, not a mere letting off of the penalty for transgression, but reconciliation and restoration, God meeting man as he turns, welcoming back the son over whose folly and estrangement He has grieved. Man's change of mind ($\mu\epsilon\tau\acute{a}\nu o\iota a$) leads to God's salvation ($\sigma\omega\tau\eta\rho\acute{\iota}a$), His rescue and restoration of man to a condition of moral health and safety. And both — man's change of mind and God's forgiveness — are effected by Jesus Christ our Lord, the Son of God made man. How is this? This is the subject for our present consideration. I would beg your careful attention while the subject is developed, as we think of our Lord's sacrifice under three aspects.

I. How does man gain this new view of himself, his duty and responsibility, and so of his failure and his sins? What gives the new motive and inspiration to change his attitude? What prompts the godly sorrow which works out repentance? All springs from a new sight of God. Man had thought of God — we too often do — as a supreme ruler, perhaps a hard taskmaster, dwelling in a distant heaven, in perfect and undisturbed bliss, indifferent to, unmoved by the sorrows, needs, and sins of His

[1] Ephesians iv. 18, ii. 2, 12.

creatures on earth.   What do these really matter to
Him? He has laid down laws, more or less arbitrary,
we think, for the regulation of man's conduct, which,
if we get caught breaking, we may have to pay a
penalty; but we will try to evade them, or hope not
to be found out, and, if caught, trust to being let off.
Is not this, crudely stated, very much the idea that
a great number of men and women entertain?

Some, turning from such a view as childish and
anthropomorphic, try to be more philosophical, and
fall into a different error on the other side, that
amounts in its consequences to much the same.   They
deprive God of all personal qualities, and regard
Him merely as the Source of all being, the animating
soul of the universe, while unconscious of the particu-
lars of our lives.   So a person once said to me, "My
God, the God of whom I think, He knows nothing
about that sorrow which has come into my life.   He
is the source of all life, but that little child that was
just given to me and then so quickly taken away
again — He of course knows nothing about that."
Such a view as this does not give much opportunity
for the godly sorrow of which St. Paul speaks.[1]

Now Jesus Christ, the incarnate Son of God, gives

[1] In his addresses to students at the Massachusetts Institute of
Technology, President Pritchett endeavors to show that it is of little
practical importance for the effect on life whether we think of
God as the infinite and eternal energy which is immanent in the
universe, — working through everlasting laws, — or whether we

us a new vision of God, of His personal being and His real character. He is the Word made flesh, God manifest in our nature. He acts out God's character in our circumstances, translates the divine perfections into language which we can understand, the language of human conduct.[1] *What Jesus was, God is.* As we see Jesus weeping by the grave of His friend Lazarus, casting a look of yearning love on the rich young man in whom He saw such possibilities, flashing with anger and indignation at the hardness of heart and hypocrisy of the Pharisees, moved with compassion for the needs of the famishing multitude, quickly ready to help the sick and sorrowful, — we learn how God regards men and things, their actions, needs, sorrows, aspirations, sins. We are certainly assured of His personal being, we learn of His interest and compassion and goodness. The Son of God took our infirmities and bare our sicknesses.[2]

Moreover, in His Passion Jesus Christ gives an object-lesson of what sin is — how God is affected by

think of Him as God our Father, an omnipotent person. *What is Religion?* pp. 40, 45, 67, 86.

Surely the difference of view must lead to widely different attitudes of mind and heart.

To introduce the idea of "arbitrary" action on the part of a personal Ruler of the universe is wholly irrelevant and misleading, as it is fallacious to suppose a necessary contradiction between God's immanence and His transcendence.

[1] John i. 1, 2, 14, 18; 1 John i. 1, 2; 2 Cor. iv. 6; 1 Tim. iii. 16.
[2] Matt. viii. 16, 17.

sin. You have seen a flashlight. For a moment a dark room was lighted up. The persons — their features and dress — the articles of furniture that before were hidden in darkness — all stand out clear. Or in a harbor the searchlight from a vessel makes clear for a moment the shipping, the pier, the docks, and fortifications. Even so the Incarnation and Passion of the Son of God show God's attitude to the world, yearning over it, drawing near, stooping down to embrace and restore man; and on the other hand, the fallen world's attitude towards God, seeking to banish and get rid of Him. God comes into this world. How is He met? Our wilfulness and disobedience reject Him. Our pride and folly would mock and blindfold Him. Our cowardice denies Him. Our hatred crucifies Him. The Incarnation and Passion of Jesus Christ make clear in the world of sense what is always true in the spiritual sphere.

Is it not something of this sort which gives interest to some sordid tragedy of which we read in the newspapers? In the squalid story there is a kind of focussing of evil, a revelation of the lengths to which evils and sins, with which we are familiar on a smaller scale or in a less conspicuous plane, may go. So in the Passion of our Lord we see our own sins writ large; it is an exhibition of the lengths to which cowardice and treachery, malice and envy, fickleness and ingratitude, may reach. We learn to hate the sins when we see their real character thus made clear, by the part they played in the crucifixion of the Son of God. In this sense, "By His stripes we are healed."[1] Thus the cross convicts man of sin. This is what sin always *is*. Now and then it is *seen* in its true character. The mind is enlightened, the conscience pricked, the heart stirred, the will moved by this spectacle. So Jesus gives repentance to Israel — to the world — to us. The prophecy is fulfilled, "They shall look on Him whom they have pierced, and they shall mourn for Him."[2] To gain compunction and repentance, then, read the story of the Lord's Passion with this thought in mind: He dies at the hands of sin.

II. But man needs more than this manifestation of sin's real character, which leads to compunction. He needs help to enable him to bring forth works

---

[1] Isaiah liii. 5, 1 Peter ii. 24. "The prophet was inspired to lay down the doctrine that no way to produce conviction of heart was so sure as that of suffering for the truth, and he was inspired to declare that this was God's foreordained plan to bring men to repentance. . . . Patience under oppression makes the oppressors consider; they recognize that such humility is more than human, and in proportion as they acknowledge the divine support given to the sufferer, they must acknowledge his goodness and their own blindness; so their eyes are opened to see the truth; by the stripes they themselves have inflicted they are themselves healed."— H. C. Beeching, *The Bible Doctrine of Atonement*, pp. 66, 67.

[2] Zechariah xii. 10.

meet for repentance, befitting this change of mind.[1]
This part also of repentance Jesus Christ gives.

He shoulders man's burden, meets our temptations, goes forth against our spiritual foes, fights out
our battle, in order to reverse the defeat we had sustained. He is the Son of God made man. In effect
He says, I will show you how you should meet temptation, how you can conquer. He allows the prince of
this world to ply Him with every kind of temptation.
In the wilderness He rejects offers of pleasure, gain,
and honor. He will not buy them at the price of
concession or compromise of duty or principle. He
will not be seduced by any of them from simple
obedience to God. In the Passion He endures threats
and assaults of pain and loss. He bares His breast
to let the enemy do his worst.[2] "You may scatter My
disciples; bring My work to disaster; heap upon Me
ignominy, insult, and misrepresentation; you may
take My bodily life: but break down My love and
loyalty, that you shall not and cannot do." In the
midst of all, in spite of all, He remains calm, unmoved, loving, pure, and brave. He is "obedient

[1] Luke iii. 8.

[2] Behind the human actors in the drama of the Passion, insti-
gating their malice and using them as instruments, we are taught
to recognize the personal activity of Satan, the prince of this world,
with whom our Lord does battle. John xiv. 30, xii. 31, Luke iv.
13, Col. ii. 15. The author may refer to his Baldwin Lectures,
Christ's Temptation and ours, Lect. II. and VI.

even unto death," even up to the surrender of His life.[1]
This is the victorious sacrifice of the cross, which we
proclaim in the Sacrament of His body and blood, in
which we glory and make our boast,[2] in which we
claim our share. It was on our behalf, as our leader
and representative, that Jesus Christ, the incarnate
Son of God, achieved this moral victory. He snapped
the bonds of sensuality and worldliness and pride,
by which men had been held down from God. He
trampled under foot the lust of the flesh, the lust of
the eyes, and the pride of life. And now we can do
the same, encouraged by His example, cheered by
His sympathy, strengthened by His grace. This idea
of a moral victory, I beg you to note, is the representation of our Lord's sacrifice most common in Holy
Scripture. This is the representation of the first gospel (as ancient writers loved to call it), the promise
of restoration recorded as given immediately after
man's sin and the imposition of his punishment.[3]
Addressing the serpent as the symbol of evil, whether
personal or impersonal, God said, '' I will put enmity

---

[1] Philippians ii. 8.

[2] 1 Corinthians xi. 26.

[3] Genesis iii. 15. It is unnecessary to enter on any discussion
of the nature or date of these early chapters of Genesis. The
point here made is that in the story at the head of the Old Testament Scriptures this representation (which doubtless colored
later thought and writing) is given of man's restoration by *rescue*
from the power of evil under which he had fallen.

between thee and the woman, between thy seed and her seed; it shall bruise thy head, and thou shalt bruise his heel." The picture is of conflict between man and the serpent. At the expense of his own heel being bruised, bitten, stung, and poisoned, in the encounter, man is to bruise and crush the serpent's head. It is an age-long conflict.[1] The prophecy does not refer exclusively to our Lord. It is the seed of the woman in general, mankind, which has to wage the war. But the victorious struggle culminates in the experience of our Lord Jesus Christ, the virgin-born, the Captain of our salvation.[2] There is no idea here of satisfaction or of propitiating an offended deity; the thought is of victory through struggle, of rescue at cost.

It is the same with our Lord's own first full representation of the nature and effect of His sacrifice in the allegory of the Good Shepherd. The Good Shepherd lays down his life for the sheep, in defending them from the attack of the beast of prey.[3]

So by a mighty effort our Lord diverts the stream of human life back into its true channel from the wrong course into which it had flowed. So He expels moral evil from the system, as something not belonging to men's nature, but fastening on it as a parasite.

---

[1] See a sermon of Phillips Brooks on "The conqueror with the wounded heel."

[2] Hebrews ii. 10.

[3] John x. 11, 15.

In St. Peter's words He redeemed us from our former
vain manner of life by His precious blood, at the cost
of His toil and pain, the shedding of His blood, the
laying down of His life.[1] He bore our sins in His own
body on the tree, that we, having died unto sin, might
live unto righteousness.[2] Thus God condemned sin
in the flesh.[3] The application of the virtue of this
victory to ourselves we shall see in the next discourse,
when we consider how we are baptized into Christ's
death, to partake of its benefits, as we make it the
law of our life. Now we are trying to make clear
Christ's death not only *by* sin, at the hands of
sin, but *to* or *from* sin. He would rather die than
yield to evil. He by death passes out of the sphere
and region of temptation. As by physical death
a man escapes from the pressure of debt, from
the prosecution of a lawsuit — he has died to or
from these experiences of life — so, following Christ's
example, we by self-denial are to pass out of
the sphere and region of temptation. In Christ
we see both God's gift and man's effort. As we
desire and struggle to be free, as we turn to God,
so He welcomes us with open arms, and breaks
the chains of sin by which we were tied and bound.
He sets us free from sin — that is Remission —
saves us not only from its guilt, but also from its
power.

[1] 1 Peter i. 17–19.   [2] 1 Peter ii. 24.   [3] Romans viii. 3.

III. At the same time Forgiveness in the narrower, more restricted sense is secured for us by Jesus Christ. We are taken out of the old life of unlove and made loving, of uncleanness and made pure, of injustice and made righteous, of falsehood and made true; but what about those old sins that we committed? How are they pardoned? Is nothing to be done about them? Shall we simply let go the past, and say no more about it?

Our old transgressions are not reckoned to us. Christ "died for our sins." He perfectly rose up to the demands of God; and further, on our behalf as the Representative of the race, He has offered a full satisfaction for all our sins, in the sense of reparation; His perfect obedience for our manifold disobedience, His spotless purity for our uncleanness, His austerity for our indulgence, His humiliation for our pride in all its various forms, His absolute self-sacrifice for our selfishness, His endurance for our weakness. This reparation, if it is not exacted by God's justice, is required by the instinct of man's loving heart. And on the strength of this we are in Christ accepted by God, and regarded with favor.

Concerning God's free forgiveness we must note two points in explanation. (1) Mankind is regarded as a whole, represented and summed up in Christ, the pattern man, the incarnate Son of God. (2) We are accepted not because we are one by one wholly worthy; God regards not merely what we are, but what we are becoming. The face is turned in the right direction, the will is surrendered. In that initial stage of germ and bud He sees the flower and fruit into which it will develop.

This reparation or satisfaction offered by our Lord on our behalf is not to be thought of as a bribe buying off the infliction of the penalty we have deserved, nor is it in any literal sense His enduring this penalty in our stead. In loving sympathy He, our elder brother, feels for us and with us. In mere earthly relationships we may have known how a father is bowed down with grief for the dishonor of his daughter; a mother's heart is broken at the disgrace and wrongdoing of her son; a wife mourns and agonizes for and with her husband in his temptation and sin; a patriot suffers in his country's loss or shame. In none of these cases is it the vicarious suffering of a substitute; it is the sympathetic grief of the loving heart for those with whom we are closely connected.

You see something of the meaning, some of the many meanings, of the general statement that "Christ died for our sins."[1] (1) He exposed Himself to sin's

[1] It is hardly necessary to say that the exposition given in this sermon makes no pretension to be an exhaustive treatment of our Lord's sacrifice and its effects. This may always remain a counsel of Divine wisdom beyond our fathoming. But the New Testa-

violence; exhibited in what it wrought on Him sin's real character and malice. (2) He wrestled with and overcame its power. (3) He offered reparation to God for its offence.

I would recommend you as you read your New Testament to do so pencil in hand, and at each mention of our Lord's sacrifice, and its effect and meaning, to write in the margin the preposition *by*, or *to*, or *for* sin, as marking the effect of His death and passion set forth in that particular passage.

ment writers (using largely, but not exclusively, the sacrificial language of the older covenant) mark out lines of thought by which we are encouraged to seek an intelligent grasp of the mystery, without venturing to say that this is the whole truth or explanation.

IV

ONE BAPTISM FOR THE
REMISSION OF SINS

IV

ONE BAPTISM FOR THE REMISSION OF SINS

After that the kindness and love of God our Saviour toward man appeared, not by works of righteousness which we have done, but according to his mercy he saved us, by the washing of regeneration, and renewing of the Holy Ghost; which he shed on us abundantly through Jesus Christ our Saviour; that being justified by his grace, we should be made heirs according to the hope of eternal life. — *Titus* iii. 4–7.

I. THIS is most probably a portion of a hymn sung in the early Christian Church. If you were to examine it in the Greek, you would see its rhythmical form and structure. There are several similar fragments of hymns quoted in St. Paul's letters,[1] especially in what are called the Pastoral Epistles (those, *i. e.*, addressed to Timothy and Titus, which are largely concerned with the duties and responsibilities of the pastoral or ministerial office), and in the Epistle to the Ephesians.[2] For instance, in Eph. v. 14 there is

---

[1] See Keble, *Sermons, Academical and Occasional*, pp. 182, 223; Liddon, Bampton Lectures, VI, p. 332 (16th ed.), where the Greek is given in verse arrangement. Also *Lauda Sion* (N. Y. Church Club Lectures), II, pp. 51–53.

[2] Ephesus (where Timothy was stationed), or at any rate Asia Minor, would seem to have been an early home of Christian hymnology. Comp. Eph. v. 19, Col. iii. 16.

4   49

a fragment of a hymn on Penitence based on Isa.
lx. 1:

> "Awake, thou that sleepest,
> and arise from the dead,
> and Christ shall shine upon thee."

In 1 Tim. i. 15 there is a fragment from a hymn on
Redemption which I have already quoted as "a faithful saying": [1]

> "Christ Jesus
> came into the world
> to save sinners."

In 1 Tim. iii. 16 there are these lines from a hymn
on our Lord's Incarnation and triumph, what we
might call an apostolic Christmas carol, concerning the mystery of godliness: [2]

> "He who was manifested in the flesh,[3]
> justified in the spirit,
> seen of angels,
> proclaimed among the nations,
> believed on in the world,
> received up in glory."

[1] The proverbial saying current in the Church. On the "faithful sayings" see J. D. James, *Genuineness and authorship of the
Pastoral Epistles*, pp. 132–136.

[2] τὸ τῆς εὐσεβείας μυστήριον, the revealed truth on which
Christian devotion is sustained.

[3] The preferable reading is ὅς (who) instead of Θεός (God).
The difference of reading makes little difference in the meaning.
The pre-existence of the subject of the lines lies in the verb "was

In 2 Tim. ii. 11–13 this "faithful saying" from a hymn on the glories of martyrdom:

> " If we died with Him, we shall also live with Him:
> if we endure, we shall also reign with Him:
> if we deny Him, He also will deny us:
> if we are faithless, He abideth faithful;
>   He cannot deny Himself."

And so this, from a hymn on the Way of Salvation:

"When the kindness of God our Saviour, and His love
    toward man, appeared,
not by works done in righteousness, which we did our-
    selves,
but according to His mercy He saved us,
through the washing of regeneration and renewing of the
    Holy Ghost,
which He poured out upon us richly, through Jesus
    Christ our Saviour;
that, being justified by His grace,
we might be made heirs according to the hope of eternal
    life." [1]

It is interesting to note these quotations. Beside the immediate teaching of each, they suggest what of

manifested." The New Testament knows of only One Being who was manifested in human form, preached among the Gentiles, taken up in glory — the Only-begotten Son. See Liddon, Pastoral Epistles, *in loc.*

[1] Notice the mention of each Person of the Blessed Trinity, as in 2 Cor. xiii. 14, which was written long before Matt. xxviii. 19.

course is the fact, though we are apt to lose sight
of it — that there were churches and congregations
of Christians, with their ministry, their stated worship, and the administration of the sacraments, their
rule of life, their struggles and triumphs, before any
of our New Testament Scriptures were written. The
apostles founded churches before they addressed
letters to them; they preached the gospel before they
committed it to writing.

To return. What in particular do we learn from
this song? What light does it throw on the general
subject of these discourses, the Forgiveness of
sins?

II. It points to the means and channel through
which God's mercy is sealed to us, His grace and
help communicated or imparted. "Through the
washing of regeneration and renewing of the Holy
Ghost,"—these are the words on which we specially
fasten our attention. Quite literally the translation
would be as in the margin of the Revised Version,
the "laver" or "bath," instead of the "washing."
The word tells rather of the place where the process
is performed than of the process itself. You remember in the Jewish tabernacle the brazen laver (made,
it was said, of the metal mirrors of the women, some
of the spoils they had carried off from Egypt), which
stood before the altar of burnt-offering, and at which

the priests were required to wash their hands and
feet before they approached God in ministry and
sacrifice.[1] With this corresponds the Font of Holy
Baptism in a Christian church (which properly
should stand near the entrance of the building). Here
we receive not a mere bodily cleansing, but a spiritual
renewal, fitting us to enter not only on the external
formal worship of the congregation, but on the whole
service of the Christian life. The passage tells, you
see, of the *one Baptism for the remission of sins*, in
which we profess our belief in the Nicene Creed.
This is our special subject for consideration in this
discourse. Let me recall to you what we have seen
hitherto about the nature of repentance, the necessary condition on man's part for receiving God's
forgiveness, the change of mind, of thought and
view, of feeling, purpose, and resolution.

We have considered the meaning of the Remission
or Forgiveness of Sins which God offers. It is no
mere letting off of a penalty, but real reconciliation
to God's favor, and restoration of our nature, that
we may become our best.

Then we saw how this was related to the sacrifice
of our Lord Jesus Christ. He offered satisfaction and
reparation for the sins of the whole world, as the
Representative of the human race on behalf of all
whom He deigned to call His brethren. And by

[1] Exodus xxx. 17–21. See Edersheim, *The Temple*, p. 130.

His victorious struggle He won our redemption, our
freedom from the bonds of sin. Now we claim our
share in this which He has accomplished for us. Its
benefits are applied to us by the ministry of His
Spirit, in the sacraments which He has ordained.
What He did for *all* is appropriated to *each*. This
is the point of sacraments. And this is why they are
administered individually, not to a congregation or
a railful, but to each person separately. "I baptize
thee"; "Defend, O Lord, *this* thy child"; "the body
of our Lord Jesus Christ, which was given for *thee*,
preserve *thy* body and soul unto everlasting life."
Among the sacraments Baptism, in which we are
made members of Christ, children of God, and
inheritors of the kingdom of heaven, holds the
primary place.

III. In the sacraments (let us be clear about this)
there is nothing mechanical or magical, as if the
outward act produced an inward effect, as if the
water poured on the body or the forehead washed
and cleansed the inner soul. That, of course, is an
entire misunderstanding of the Church's teaching.
A sacrament is an outward and visible sign of an
inward and spiritual grace, which, if we approach
with right dispositions, accompanies the outward
sign. Each part, the outward sign and the inward
gift, is real in its own sphere; the outward sign for

our outer nature, the inward gift for our inner being. The outward sign is, as the Catechism teaches
us, both the means whereby we receive the inward
gift, and a pledge to assure us thereof.[1] Thus you
see the institution of sacraments is true to our two-
fold nature, physical and spiritual. These different
elements of our complex being are very closely and
intimately linked together. Our whole life, we may
say, is sacramental. Our thought is expressed in
words; a wish is signified by a glance; affection is
shown in a kiss; the grasp of the hand is a token of
confidence. In imparting to us, then, great spiritual
gifts for our inner life in connection with and by
means of outward signs God is recognizing the two-
fold character of the nature which He has fashioned.
Baptism does not consist in the outer washing. It
is not, as St. Peter says, the putting away of the
filth of the flesh, but the appeal of a good conscience
towards God.[2]

[1] See Hooker, *Eccles. Pol.*, VI. vi. 10: "So God hath instituted
and ordained, that, together with due administration and receipt
of sacramental signs, there shall proceed from Himself grace
effectual to sanctify, to cure, to comfort, and whatsoever else is for
the good of the souls of men."

Compare the comment of Thomas Aquinas on Acts viii. 18,
which Hooker quotes in the same chapter: "Manus impositio non
causat Spiritus Sancti adventum; sed simul cum manus imposi-
tione Spiritus Sanctus advenit. Unde non dicitur in textu quod
Apostoli imponentes manus darent Spiritum Sanctum, sed quod
imponebant manus, et illi accipiebant Spiritum Sanctum."

[2] 1 Pet. iii. 21, ἐπερώτημα. Dr. Pusey sees in this word an

IV. What I desire particularly to insist on is this: that Baptism represents both man's Repentance and God's Forgiveness; our desire to be freed, and God's setting us free; our desire to begin over again, and God's giving us a fresh start; our putting away of sin, and God's putting it away from us; our gift of ourselves to Him, and God's acceptance of the gift, taking us to Himself as members of His family, and imparting to us His moral nature.[1]   In a word, God enables as to carry out the desire He has put into our minds.

Consider how each part — Repentance and Remission — is expressed in Baptism.

1. The promises represent and express our change of mind and view. We ask now, What is right, what is God's will? not, What should I like to do, or what will bring me gain? Before the vows of Belief and Obedience, which mark the surrender of ourselves to God, there comes the promise of Renunciation of God's enemies and ours, to whom by nature we were subject, whom too often we have actually obeyed, who largely rule in the world around.[2] In the legal process of naturalization a person com-

allusion to the interrogations in Baptism, which were to be answered by a faith unfeigned. — *Tract on Baptism*, p. 8. It may more probably be translated "seeking after" God by the inner man, drawing near to receive His gift of spiritual cleansing in the sacramental washing.

[1] 2 Peter i. 4.   [2] Ephesians ii. 2, 1 John v. 19.

ing from another country, and desiring to become a citizen of the United States, before he is admitted to the privileges of citizenship is called upon first to renounce allegiance to any foreign prince or potentate, and in particular to the one from whose jurisdiction the applicant comes — for instance, the German Kaiser, the Czar of Russia, the King of Great Britain and Ireland, or the French Republic. He is then called upon further to disavow certain special evils which are recognized as dangerous to the commonwealth. He must declare, "I am not an anarchist, I am not a polygamist, nor do I believe in the practice of polygamy."

So in Baptism we renounce and break away from the Devil and his works, the World and its pomps and vanities — all, personal or impersonal, that comes between us and God, and the Flesh with its sinful and unregulated desires.

2. This renunciation on our part is sealed by the act of Baptism. This signifies our desire to be freed from the guilt of old transgressions and from the power of evil — to put it all away. And our Repentance is met by God's act. He, through the ordinance that He has appointed, bestows upon us the washing of regeneration and renewing of the Holy Spirit.[1] It is, you see, the common act of God

---

[1] The renewal by the Holy Spirit (which is a constant process) as distinct from regeneration (which is a single act) may belong

and of man. Washing requires co-operation. A child may resist its mother's attempt, may run away from the bath; we must yield ourselves, our inner nature, to be cleansed. My hand is stained, I desire to have it cleansed; it is put into the water; but for effectual cleansing it must be rubbed and scrubbed by the other hand. Even so there is need of God's action to meet and carry out our desire.

V. This same thought is represented by the other idea in Baptism. We are baptized, St. Paul says, into Christ's death.[1] The font is a tomb, where with Christ we die *from* or *to* sin. The administration of Baptism by immersion sets forth, of course, far more vividly this symbolism of burial with Christ than

more strictly to what we call Confirmation than to the actual Baptism; but in early times the two ceremonies were regarded rather as two parts of one sacrament than as entirely separate ordinances. See Mason, *The Relation of Confirmation to Baptism*, pp. 1, 49.

[1] Rom. vi. 2–12; comp. 1 Peter iv. 1–5. "Just as Christ summed up His attitude towards the world by His death upon the cross, so the Christian's attitude to the world was summed up in his baptism. At that moment he died to the world of sin. This state of deadness to sin has to be constantly renewed, or again and again recovered. But it was in that sacramental moment realized in principle and symbolically represented. The convert who was immersed beneath the baptismal waters and emerged again, realized easily that this 'bath of regeneration' was, what the early Christians called it, 'his grave and his mother.'"—Bp. Gore, *Practical Exposition of the Epistle to the Romans*, i. p. 214.

does Baptism by pouring water on the person. But
we have no reason to suppose that the efficacy of the
sacrament depends on the amount of water used.

Both by our desire and by God's enabling grace
the Christian dies to sin; he breaks away from it,
and gets out of its sphere. "He that is dead is freed
from sin." Physical death frees a man from civil
prosecution. He has passed beyond the jurisdiction of the legal officers. So should our union
with Christ's death remove us from the dominion of
evil. A person's name is found on the tax-list or on
the roll of some society. He is invited to a banquet,
or summoned to pay a tax. "He is dead," it is re-
ported, "he cannot come." Even so it ought to be
said of a baptized Christian, when some temptation
to evil is suggested, "He is dead; he cannot join in
that revelry, or dishonesty, or slander."

This, some one may say, is all very well. It is
doubtless the Bible standard, and the teaching of the
Prayer-book; but is it practicable? Now, let us
remember, neither in the Bible nor in the Prayer-
book is it represented that this death to sin is done
once for all. "Baptism doth represent unto us our
profession; which is, to follow the example of our
Saviour Christ, and to be made like unto him; that,
as he died, and rose again for us, so should we, who
are baptized, die from sin, and rise again unto righteousness; *continually* mortifying all our evil and

corrupt affections, and *daily* proceeding in all virtue
and godliness of living." [1] It is a life of renunciation
which at Baptism we entered on. There must be a
daily dying to sin. The mode of Christ's actual
death, which is the pattern of our death to evil, sets
this forth. At the block a single stroke sufficed; at
the stake the flames soon touched a vital part; but
crucifixion was a slow and lingering death. We are
in Baptism fastened to the cross, our sinful nature
doomed to death; all our life in this world we must
be true to this law of spiritual life through death.
We enter into its meaning and realize its force more
and more. We lose our lower life in order to gain
our higher life. We let go passing pleasures and
gains in order that we may lay hold of those which
are really worthy and enduring.

To return to the illustration of naturalization. A
man has renounced his old citizenship. It was not
altogether bad, but (as we at any rate think) poor
when compared with the privileges and responsibilities
of our free country. Take the case of a Russian or
a Pole; he enters in America on a new kind of life;
not only beneath new skies, and with a different
climate and surroundings, but with largely a different

[1] Exhortation at end of the Baptismal office. "Baptism into
His death and resurrection for us is nothing except as it is also and
equally baptism into our dying and rising with Him."—Du Bose,
Gospel in St. Paul, p. 178.

mental and moral atmosphere, with larger liberties, wider opportunities, more serious responsibilities. He gains the new in exchange for the old which he gives up. And he grows by degrees in realization and appreciation of the new conditions. He does not appreciate this all at once, nor in the first years of his coming among us. So in the Christian life we are to realize more and more what our Baptism meant for us:

(a) Its privileges and graces and helps, — (i.) forgiveness for the past, and the promise of continued forgiveness; (ii.) acceptance with God in Christ our head, as members of His body; (iii.) the pledged help of the Holy Spirit for the future; (iv.) fellowship in the Church, the Christian society, the family of God, the brotherhood of the disciples; (v.) the being taken out of the old evil course and placed in the Way of salvation, with guideposts along the road :[1]

(b) And on the other hand its corresponding responsibilities and obligations — to live true to this call, to use these gifts.

Examine yourselves, brethren, whether ye be in the faith.[2] Seek to live worthy of the vocation wherewith ye are called.[3]

[1] "The Way" was a common expression in apostolic times for the Christian religion. See Acts ix. 2, xix. 9, 23, xxiv. 14, 22.

[2] 2 Corinthians xiii. 5.

[3] Ephesians iv. 1.

V

THE FORGIVENESS OF SINS
AFTER BAPTISM

V

THE FORGIVENESS OF SINS AFTER BAPTISM

Is any among you afflicted? let him pray. Is any merry? let him sing psalms. Is any sick among you? let him call for the elders of the church; and let them pray over him, anointing him with oil in the name of the Lord: and the prayer of faith shall save the sick, and the Lord shall raise him up; and if he have committed sins, they shall be forgiven him. Confess your faults one to another, and pray one for another, that ye may be healed. The supplication of a righteous man availeth much in its working.

James v. 13–16.

I. In the last discourse we considered the symbolism and significance of Baptism, the "one Baptism for the remission of sins," in which we profess our belief in the Nicene Creed. It represents the putting away of sin, of moral evil. The washing of the body is the outward and visible sign of the cleansing of our inner nature — our mind and heart, our conscience and will — by the Spirit of God. But the putting away of evil is represented by more than by washing. The font is not only a bath or laver; it is a place of burial. We are "baptized into Christ's death," to share its benefits and to obey its law. "We are buried with Him through baptism into death," that with Him we may die to sin, the world, and self, and rise to newness of life. This is what

5 65

Baptism symbolizes, as the Catechism puts it, "a death unto sin, and a new birth unto righteousness."

On two points about this I desire to insist, even at the expense of some repetition, for one of them we considered with some fulness in the last discourse.

First, then, the putting away of evil in Baptism is *both man's act and God's*. God does not act in spite of us or apart from us, in any mechanical fashion. Baptism is administered on the condition of our Repentance and Faith. For our part we renounce and promise to fight against God's enemies and our own, the Devil, the World, and the Flesh. We surrender ourselves to God for obedience in faith and life. We submit to the sacred washing; we enroll ourselves as servants and soldiers of Christ crucified. That is our part. And then for His part, God (who Himself prompts these good desires) meets and welcomes us as we turn to Him; He gives grace and help to accomplish that which we desire, and which the sacrament symbolizes.

" Not by works done in righteousness, which we did ourselves,
　but according to His mercy He saved us,
　through the washing of regeneration and renewing of the Holy Ghost,
　which He poured out upon us richly, through Jesus Christ our Saviour."

This is one point, the co-operation between God and man, that is involved in Baptism.

Here is the second point, equally important for us to remember, and especially with reference to the particular subject of this discourse. The covenant concerning the putting away of sin — our Repentance or change of mind, and God's Forgiveness or Remission — is on both sides an enduring agreement, a lasting promise. We promise obediently to keep God's holy will and commandments, and to walk in the same *all the days of our life*. God bestows upon us the *everlasting* benediction of His heavenly washing. On neither side — this is the point — is it something done and finished once for all.

Baptism (so we have thought of it) is an initiation into a new sphere of life, under new conditions. It is a new birth. New life is once communicated or started, but it is continually preserved; and its maintenance depends largely on our obedience to the laws of health. The immigrant from a foreign country is at a definite time admitted by naturalization to the rights of citizenship. The country then becomes his home; for the remainder of his years he is entitled to its privileges and protection; he is bound by its laws.

So it is with the kingdom of heaven, the Christian society. We have promised to obey its laws, to fight against its enemies; we are bound to use our best endeavors to enlarge its borders, and spread its influence. On these conditions we are admitted to its spiritual privileges. In Christ we are welcomed to God's favor; our past sins are pardoned and blotted out; the assistance of the Holy Spirit is pledged to us. The only difference in this regard between the earthly society and the heavenly is this: that the privileges and obligations of the one end with our natural life, while the blessings of the other are only entered upon, and, as it were, tasted here; they are to receive their full development hereafter. We look for the life of the world to come. But in either case the privileges are enduring, and the obligations are lifelong.

Physical birth, initiation into a society, naturalization in a country, spiritual regeneration, — none of these are repeated. They form the groundwork, the starting point, for all that follows, in growth, in promotion, in holding of office, in privilege and service.

There is then "one Baptism for the remission of sins." This is the base of our whole Christian life. To this we must be continually recurring. It cannot be repeated. There should be a growing realization of its privileges and its obligations. The new gift of the Spirit of God in Confirmation is a sealing of our Baptism. The spiritual food of the Holy Communion is for the nourishment of the new life of

Christ imparted to us at Baptism. Having in Baptism been made "members of Christ, children of God, and inheritors of the kingdom of heaven," we have freedom of approach to God as members of His adopted family. The Remission or putting away of sins pledged to us in Baptism refers not only to past sins, whether original or actual; it extends to our daily faults. Our sins of infirmity are mercifully pardoned. God makes allowance for the frailty of His children. As reconciled and adopted children we are taught by Christ Himself to ask continually, as often as we repeat the Lord's Prayer, that our heavenly Father would "forgive us our trespasses," on the condition, of course, of continued penitence and renewed sorrow on our part, manifested in our forgiveness of those who have wronged us. In the public worship of the congregation His mercy and pardon are called down upon us in authoritative prayers and absolutions.[1]

This is the ideal of the Christian life, a development and growth in grace as in nature, an onward and upward progress in spite of slips and lesser faults. As in nature so in grace there is a recuperative power in life to throw off minor hurts and ailments, as distinct from serious diseases or injuries,

---

[1] Having been bathed, we need only — but this we do need — to wash our feet from the dust that soils us on our homeward path. John xiii. 10.

which threaten to destroy the life itself. These may
need more thorough and even painful treatment.[1]

II. This, I say, is the ideal of the Christian life, —
development and growth with no grave falling away.
But what if this should occur? What if a baptized
Christian by some grievous sin or course of sin, by
continued carelessness and indifference, has really
fallen away from his baptismal position? He has
broken the vows of renunciation that he made, and
yielded himself to the Devil and his works, to the
World and its ways, to the Flesh and the indulgence
of its sinful lusts; he has disregarded his promises of
faith and obedience. Such a one, instead of dying
to the world, and continually mortifying all evil and
corrupt affections, has died to higher and spiritual
interests. He has withdrawn from the guidance and
control of the Holy Spirit; he has practically renounced discipleship to Christ; he has fallen out of
fellowship and favor with God.

How is he, when he comes to a better mind, to be
dealt with? He may have been formally separated,

---

[1] So Salvian, quoted by Hooker, *Eccles. Pol.*, VI. iv. 6. "These
[high and capital offences, as denial of the faith, perjury, fornica-
tion, murder, sorcery] and such like committed crimes cannot
thoroughly be taken away with ordinary, moderate, and secret
satisfaction; but greater causes do require greater and sharper
remedies; they need such remedies as are not only sharp, but
solemn, open, and public." — Hom. x.

on account of his wrongdoing, from the company of the faithful, or at least suspended from its highest privileges in the Holy Communion.[1] In days of stricter discipline he would have been so dealt with, for his own good as well as for the good of others.[2] Such a person needs restoration to the position which he has forfeited. First, of course, he must show the reality and earnestness of his penitence, of his renewed change of mind; he must make such restitution and amends as are possible for the injury he has done to others, by example and influence, if in no other way. In days of discipline a set time and opportunity would have been appointed, like the season of Lent, in which a person's penitence should be tested and manifested. And then with the prayers of the Church and the absolution of its minister and representative (acting on behalf of the whole body) he would be restored and replaced in the position he had forfeited.[3]

The absolution, remember, has a two-fold purpose and effect. (1) It is a bringing home to the individual of God's promise of pardon and forgive-

[1] For the distinction between the lesser excommunication (which deprives of sacraments) and the greater (which cuts off from Christian fellowship) see the author's charge on *Ecclesiastical Discipline*, p. 12, note.

[2] See W. Bright, *Some Aspects of Primitive Church Life*, p. 137.

[3] See Marshall's *Penitential Discipline* (in the Anglo-Catholic Library).

ness, after others (who would be impartial) have had an opportunity to judge of the person's repentance, that it satisfies the conditions required for forgiveness. (2) It is, moreover, a putting forth of spiritual power [1] for the person's release from the bondage of evil to which he had yielded himself. It sets free again the flow of spiritual life which had been choked by the obstruction of sin. [2]

All, of course, is done in the name of God, by His delegated authority, even as our Lord declared that the Son of man had authority on earth to forgive sins, and then commissioned His apostles to act in His name: "As My Father sent Me, even so send I you." [3]

[1] By way of prayer offered by representatives of the body of Christ.

[2] It is of great importance clearly to keep in mind that Absolution depends entirely upon the baptismal covenant already made. There is required, implicitly at least, the renewal of his baptismal promises by the penitent. Absolution is his restoration to his baptismal position and privileges. Strictly speaking, no *new* gift is bestowed in Absolution, as in Baptism, Confirmation, Communion, or Ordination; the life of Baptism is renewed, or set free.

[3] Mark ii. 10, John xx. 21–23. Referring to Matt. xvi. 19 Hooker says, "This is that grand original warrant, by force whereof the guides and prelates in God's Church, first his Apostles, and afterwards others following them successively, did both use and uphold that discipline, the end whereof is to heal men's consciences, to cure their sins, to reclaim offenders from iniquity, and to make them by repentance just." — *Eccles. Pol.*, VI, iv. 1.

The commission was given not to the original twelve only. See Bp. Andrewes, "Of the power of Absolution," sermons, vol. V,

And all is subject to His ratification or reversal, according as He, who alone can read our hearts, sees whether the person really has the right dispositions for pardon and reconciliation.

Two points especially I would ask you to note.

1. God acts through His minister in Absolution as in Baptism.[1] It is His act whether the priest says, "I baptize thee" or "I absolve thee."[2] Both Baptism

p. 91: "This was no personal privilege to be in the Apostles and to die with them, that they should only execute it for a time, and none ever after them. God forbid we should so think of it. For this power being more than needful for the world, . . . it was not to be either personal or for a time. Then those persons dying, and those times determining, they in the ages following, as we now in this, that should light into this prison or captivity of sin, how could they or we receive any benefit by it? Of nature it was said by the heathen philosopher that it doth neither *abundare in superfluis*, nor *deficere in necessariis*. God forbid but we should ascribe as much to God at the least, that neither He would ordain a power superfluous or more than needed, or else it being needful would appropriate it unto one age, and leave all other destitute of it; and not rather as all writers both new and old take it, continue it successively to the world's end."

[1] So St. Ambrose (arguing against the Novatians): "Cur baptizatis, si per hominem peccata dimitti non licet? In Baptismo utique remissio peccatorum omnium est. Quid interest utrum per poenitentiam, an per lavacrum hoc jus sibi sacerdotes vindicent? Unum in utroque mysterium est." — *De Poenitentia*, I, 8.

[2] Absolution in early times was undoubtedly given in a precatory form, like that in our order for Holy Communion. The indicative form is, I think, first found in Egbert's Pontifical, A.D. 767, and did not come into general use until the 13th century. Both the precatory and the indicative are combined in the English

and Absolution are appointed means through which God seals to us the forgiveness of our sins, and the assurance of our acceptance with Him, when apart from any such pledge a penitent might be left in distress, doubting whether his repentance were sufficient.

2.   Absolution is an illustration of the social character of the Christian religion. We are not intended to seek God and His gifts as isolated units, each for himself and by himself. We are gathered into a family, we are made members of a body. In the Christian brotherhood we are to give and receive help one to and one from another. Our varying gifts, whether personal or official, are for the common good.[1] "Confess your faults one to another, and pray one for another, that ye may be healed," says St. James. And if "to one another," then certainly not least to one who is trained and appointed to act as a spiritual pastor and physician, a guide of souls.[2]

This exercise of discipline and restoration, of re-

form for private Absolution, "Our Lord Jesus Christ . . . of His great mercy forgive thee thine offences; And by His authority . . . I absolve thee from all thy sins." The indicative form was probably at first understood to apply to reconciliation to the Church, while the precatory was what procured from God the penitent's pardon. See Marshall, *Penitential Discipline*, pp. 144–153.

[1] 1 Cor. xii. 7.

[2] So Hooker, *Eccl. Pol.*, VI, iv. 7.

taining and remitting sins, we see illustrated by St. Paul in his dealing with the Corinthians. In his first epistle to Corinth we hear of a grievous scandal in the Christian society. A member of the Church had fallen into a horrible sin of immorality. And there was a general laxity on the part of the Church in tolerating the evil, and in failing to bear witness to true Christian standards. The apostle decides that the offender, for the good of the society, and for his own soul's sake, must be separated from the company of the faithful. Acting along with the Church at Corinth, in the name of the Lord Jesus Christ and by His power, he separates the evil-doer from Christian privileges, hands him over (by withdrawing from him the spiritual protection of the Church) to Satan for the destruction of the flesh, that his spirit may be saved in the day of the Lord Jesus.[1]

Here is an instance of the *retaining* of sins by an apostle, — not, mark you, by one to whom our Lord Jesus Christ had Himself given the commission while He was on the earth, but by one who was admitted by Christ from heaven to the same office with the original twelve. Then in the second epistle we have an instance of St. Paul's *remitting* the sins of one who had been proved truly penitent. It matters not for our present purpose whether it was the same offender, or another person who had sinned in a different man-

[1] 1 Cor. v. 1-5.

ner. "To whom ye forgive anything," the apostle
writes, "I forgive also; for if I forgave anything, to
whom I forgave it, for your sakes forgave I it in the
person of Christ." And he adds a reason of spiritual
prudence, "that no advantage may be gained over us
by Satan," in driving the excommunicated offender
into recklessness and despair. Accordingly he bids
the brethren now forgive the offender who had
proved his repentance, and comfort him, lest he
should be swallowed up by overmuch sorrow.[1]

Such is the normal mode of dealing with a lapsed
Christian. On his repentance he is restored by a
ministerial act in Absolution to that position in which
by a ministerial act he was placed at his Baptism,
but out of which by grievous sin he had fallen.

III. But apart from any formal exercise of ecclesiastical authority, there are many cases where persons of their own accord may submit themselves to
penitential exercises.[2] They desire to unburden

[1] 2 Cor. ii. 6–11.

[2] Hooker, *Eccles. Pol.*, VI, iv. 7. Hooker speaks in early times
of "Offenders in secret, knowing themselves altogether unworthy
to be admitted to the Lord's table, as the others which were with-
held," voluntarily submitting to the same discipline. He shows
how after the conversion of the Roman empire, and the consequent
lowering of the standard of Christian life, voluntary penitents
were restrained from open confession for fear of scandal, and
private confession took its place, continuing "as a profitable ordinance " in the Western Church, until the fourth Lateran Council

themselves by a special and detailed confession of their sins to or before God's priest (who represents both God and the Church), and then to seek from him an authoritative, ministerial absolution.

There are (believe one who has had considerable experience) many more cases of uneasy and burdened consciences than you might suppose. There are cases where some sin of past years is exerting a blighting influence on the spiritual life, keeping a person back from Communion, preventing peace of mind, depriving him of that peace and joy in believing which should be a characteristic of the Christian life. There are other cases where some entangling habit of evil baffles the person's best endeavors to get free. Such a one very often supposes his condition to be unique and beyond hope. He needs encouragement and guidance from one who has had experience, with sympathy and help from a spiritual friend. "If only," a person says, "I could tell out my grief to some one whom I could trust; if I could take shame to myself by the acknowledgment of what I have done; if I could be true to some one, and so get rid of that horrible feeling of hypocrisy, when others, who do not know the facts, think well and speak kindly of me; if only I might have the assurance of some

(1215) made it obligatory at least once in a year (iv. 2). He shows also how private confession existed alongside of the public discipline (iv. 7).

impartial judge that my repentance now is such as God will accept, — what an inexpressible relief it would be!" Now it belongs to the priest and spiritual pastor to minister to such cases. It is his duty and privilege to hold up the weak, to heal the sick, and bind up the broken, as well as to bring again the outcast, and seek the lost. We must get rid of the miserable notion that a clergyman's duty is only or chiefly to conduct the public worship of the congregation and to preach sermons; he is commissioned to feed the sheep, to tend the lambs, and rule the flock. His office consists not only in general persuasions unto amendment of life, addressed to the congregation, but also in the private, particular cure of diseased minds.[1] We have our individual temptations, sins, needs, doubts, and difficulties, yes, and (thank God!) our individual aspirations and yearnings. In all we need or may claim individual and personal help of a spiritual physician and guide of souls.

It is along these lines that we are to understand the exhortation of St. James at the end of his epistle. Under all circumstances he bids Christians turn to God in prayer: Is any among you suffering? let him pray. Is any cheerful? let him sing praise. Is any among you sick? let him call for the elders, that is, the presbyters, of the Church (they are sent for as

---

[1] Hooker, as quoted above.

representatives of the Christian brotherhood, and as
presumably themselves men of piety); and let them
pray over him, anointing him with oil in the name of
the Lord (we cannot here discuss this clause: it
probably means, *either* using the ordinary means for
recovery of health, to which they were to add their
prayers, *or* using a symbolical ceremony that told of
that bodily healing for which they prayed)[1]: and the
prayer of faith shall save him that is sick, and the
Lord shall raise him up (that is, of course, if God
sees that the restoration of the person's health would
be really for his good); and then the apostle adds
further, If he be one who has committed sins, if this
be his condition, that of a sinner, if there be sins by
which his conscience is oppressed, sins that perhaps,
in part at least, were the cause of his sickness, then
forgiveness or absolution shall be extended to him.
(That is distinctly the meaning of the Greek, in which
St. James wrote.[2]) Then he concludes with a general exhortation suggested by this, Confess, therefore,
your faults one to another, and pray one for another,[3]
that ye may be healed of bodily or spiritual sickness.

---

[1] On the Anointing of the Sick, see Note at the end.

[2] κἂν ἁμαρτίας ᾖ πεποιηκώς, ἀφεθήσεται αὐτῷ, and if he be in
the state of having committed weighty sins in the past, the effects
of which remain, remission shall be imparted to him.

[3] ἐξομολογεῖσθε οὖν ἀλλήλοις τὰς ἁμαρτίας, καὶ εὔχεσθε ὑπὲρ
ἀλλήλων, *i. e.* all in their turn, as occasion shall call for it. Comp.
Eph. v. 21, "be subject one to another." So Marshall, pp. 80, 81,

The supplication (by way of intercession) of a righteous man availeth much in its working.

IV. In connection with all that has been said, I
beg you to remember three cautions, that you may
not carry away any wrong or mistaken impression.

1. I need hardly say that Confession without
Repentance is of no value. It would be a grievous
wrong, and a most dangerous snare. It is only as the
expression of a genuine repentance that confession can
be of any avail. Confession to a priest is not in the
place of confession to God; it is a further step, after
having confessed one's sins privately to God, to confess them to Him in the presence of His minister.
This may help us to definiteness of self-knowledge,
calling our sins by their true names before another,
as it will help us to realize the shame of the wrong
we have done. It may procure for us the definite
advice of which we stand in need, as well as the benefit of absolution.

2. I am not here and now concerned with any
rule for the habitual practice of confession at stated
times. That is an entirely distinct question. It may
or may not be advantageous in different cases. What
I am speaking of is the confession of sins before God's
priest when occasion and need demand.

3. In the matter of special Confession and Absolution there is no question of compulsion, in the

absence of authoritative discipline. The Church leaves us free. This we may say (and I am using the words of a learned and venerable English bishop [1]): The Church of England says to her *priests*, you *must* be ready to hear the confessions of persons who seek this help; she says to her *people*, You *may make* a special confession, if you desire to do so for your own peace of mind and for the deepening of your penitence.[2]

In conclusion I would say this: Do not scorn (even if you do not feel its need) this gracious provision which God has left in His Church for the relief

---

[1] Dr. King, Bishop of Lincoln.

[2] Against the obligation of confession as urged by the Roman Church, see Hooker, *Eccles. Pol.*, VI, iv. 4, 6, 13, 16 (quoting St. Chrysostom), vi. 2, 17. In a valuable discussion of "The Penitential Discipline of the Church," printed in the *Guardian* for Nov. 9 and 16, 1898, Dr. Gore says: Private confession is intended by the Church to be "thoroughly voluntary; and not merely in the sense in which all religious acts are worthless which do not involve an act of will. In the latter sense, Communion is voluntary. Auricular confession is voluntary in the further sense that the Church requires no one to make it unless their own conscience urges them to. It is not the only method accepted by the Church of recovery from every grievous sin, but *one* method. It is our business to see that all Churchmen know of its existence and meaning. . . . But we are bound also not to go beyond our commission. We are bound to hear the confessions of those who come to make them. But we are bound also — not only to refuse to make confession a formal requisite for Confirmation or Communion, but — not to represent it as practically necessary." — *Guardian*, LIII, pt. ii, p. 1781.

6

of sin-sick souls. Do not, I would most earnestly beg of you, be kept back through fear or shame from seeking such help, if you feel its need. It is shameful to commit sin; but to acknowledge it with sorrow and repudiation, that is not shameful, but noble. Men, not angels, are ministers of the Gospel. The one before whom you make your confession is a fellow sinner, a fellow suppliant, and a fellow penitent. "If a man be overtaken in a fault," says St. Paul, "ye which are spiritual (he is probably referring more particularly to the clergy as having the spiritual cure of souls), restore such an one in the spirit of meekness, considering thyself, lest thou also be tempted." [1]

And do not dare, by dissuasion or influence or ridicule, to keep back any who desire this help from seeking it, because you do not feel the need yourself.

Let not those who are satisfied with their own personal confession to God, and with the general confession in the congregation, be offended with those who use, to their further satisfying, special confession before a priest.[2] Let us all see to this, that our word

[1] Gal. vi. 1. Jeremy Taylor understands "the spiritual man" to be "the curate of souls." *Doctrine and Practice of Repentance*, IX, ii.

[2] This was the wise and charitable exhortation in the Warning before Holy Communion in the first English Prayer-book (1549): "And if there be any of you whose conscience is troubled and grieved in anything, lacking comfort or counsel, let him come to

of repentance, our confession, however made — in our private prayers, in the public service, before another — be such a true expression of the heart of repentance, the godly sorrow, the broken and contrite heart which God will not despise, that it may win His forgiveness. If, with true repentance, we confess our sins, God is faithful and just to forgive us our sins, and to cleanse us from all unrighteousness.

me or to some other discreet and learned Priest, taught in the law of God, and confess and open his sin and grief secretly, that he may receive such ghostly counsel, advice, and comfort, that his conscience may be relieved: And that of us (as the ministers of God and of the Church) he may receive comfort and absolution to the satisfaction of his mind and avoiding of all scruple and doubtfulness: requiring such as shall be satisfied with a general confession not to be offended with them that do use to their further satisfying the auricular and secret confession to the Priest; nor those also which think needful and convenient for the guidance of their consciences particularly to open their sins to the Priest, to be offended with them that are satisfied with their humble confession to God and the general confession to the Church. But in all things to follow and keep the rule of charity, and every man to be satisfied with his own conscience, not judging other men's minds or consciences, whereas he hath no warrant of God's word to the same."

VI

REMAINING CONSEQUENCES OF
FORGIVEN SINS

VI

REMAINING CONSEQUENCES OF FORGIVEN SINS

David said unto Nathan, I have sinned against the LORD. And
Nathan said unto David, The LORD also hath put away thy sin;
thou shalt not die. Howbeit, because by this deed thou hast given
great occasion to the enemies of the LORD to blaspheme, the child
also that is born unto thee shall surely die. Now therefore the
sword shall never depart from thine house; because thou hast
despised me, and hast taken the wife of Uriah the Hittite to be
thy wife. *2 Samuel* xii. 13, 14, and 10.

WHEN I was first in San Francisco twenty-five
years ago, I was told that shortly before my visit a
club of professional gentlemen of the city — lawyers,
doctors, merchants, and so forth — at one of their
literary and social meetings had arranged what they
called "A Trial of King David." They had counsel
for the prosecution and counsel for the defence, a
judge and a jury. A verdict was returned, and a sentence passed, far more severe and (as they thought)
far more just than that meted out to David by
Almighty God in Holy Scripture. The gentlemen
were disposed to boast of their higher morality, at any
rate with regard to others' offences. How far they
practised what they preached I had no opportunity
of learning. This I know, that with a good many
men and women, in eastern as well as western com-

munities, the estimate of crime depends in considerable measure upon whether it is found out or not.

I. However, it is not my purpose to dwell on this now. Nor will I do more than mention a point which certainly must not be lost sight of if we would judge righteous judgment. It is this, that David, with all his personal advantages, is not to be judged by Christian standards. Men and women living under the older dispensation, remember, had never seen the perfect example of human life given by Jesus Christ our Lord; they had never heard the lofty moral teaching of the Sermon on the Mount; nor had they received the gift of the indwelling Spirit of God such as is pledged to us at our Confirmation. They had not been made members of Christ, children of God, inheritors of the kingdom of heaven. He that is least in the kingdom of heaven (the Christian Church), said our Lord Himself, is greater in privilege than the highest of prophets and representatives of the Old Testament. They belonged to an earlier stage in the world's moral education.[1]

It follows, you will recognize, that *we* ought to surpass the virtues which are conspicuous in God's servants in the older time. The faith of Abraham, the obedience of Isaac, the prayer of Jacob, the purity of Joseph, the courage and unworldliness of

[1] Matthew xi. 11, Hebrews vi. 4, xi. 39, 40.

Daniel, and the penitence of David ought to be re-produced and surpassed by us with our greater and higher gifts.   Their faults and failings furnish little excuse for us in our more favored position.

This, too, is by the way.   What I want to dwell on, in connection with the special subject of the last of our Lenten discourses, is the great illustration given in David's case that consequences often remain to be borne after sins have been forgiven.

II.   After his dreadful sin, on the horror of which, with all its aggravations, we need not now enlarge, David has been won to repentance.   He has learned that sins are not forgiven because they are forgotten, that there is no sacrament of oblivion, such as we often trust to.   David forgets, and Bathsheba for-gets; but the just and holy God would not have it so.   David had lulled his conscience.   For over nine months, nearly a year, he went on as usual, carrying on the affairs of the kingdom, attending the services in the Tabernacle.   Sin blinds as well as binds.   It dulls the conscience, while it cripples the will.   This is true, remember, of fraud and dishonesty, of any evil habit, as well as of sensual indulgence.

But God in mercy did not cast him off.   He re-members us when we forget Him, even when we try to forget Him.   He calls, and recalls, when we wander, and calls again, and then receives us on our return.

He does not easily let go. So He sends Nathan, the friend of earlier days, to David. His very presence revives old memories. And Nathan tells his touching parable of the rich man who spared to take of his own flocks and herds to prepare for the traveller, but seized the pet lamb of his tenant, and dressed it for his guest. Ah, those Bible stories, how they find us out! how true they are to nature, to the facts of human life! Listen to David's hard, quick censures. David passes a severe sentence: "The man that hath done this thing is surely deserving of death." We have open eyes, sharp tongues for the faults of others, while often we are blind and easy toward ourselves.

Then Nathan drives home the conviction of sin. "*Thou* art the man." He upbraids David in the name of God for his wickedness and ingratitude; he reminds him what God had done for him, what favors He had shown him. And *this* is the return. Then David sobs out his confession. It bursts upon him what he has done, the wrong to others — to Bathsheba, to Uriah, to Joab (whom he had drawn into the plot), to his subjects (whom he had scandalized), and against God who had laid down the law, and established and hallowed the relationships that he had violated, between man and woman, between sovereign and people; against God who had shown him such favors and exalted him from his low estate to be king over His chosen people. "I have sinned against the Lord."

The absolution follows quick upon the word of penitence. There is pardon for all sin on due and proportionate repentance. Though sins be as scarlet, they shall be as white as snow; though they be red like crimson, they shall be as wool.[1] "If we confess our sins, God is faithful and just to forgive us our sins, and to cleanse us from all unrighteousness."[2] "The Lord also hath put away thy sin; thou shalt not die." The word of pardon, you see, is brought home by God's messenger to the penitent, who could hardly otherwise have realized its possibility and truth.

III. But this was not all that Nathan said. He did not stop here. This was what the San Francisco gentlemen forgot. They thought that David got off too easily. We not infrequently hear the same kind of remarks. The president of a New England college is said to have declared that preachers might come to the college and preach anything they pleased except about King David; any mention of him he could not stand. It is a shallow criticism, based on a superficial reading of Scripture. "Howbeit," Nathan went on, "because by this deed thou hast given great occasion to the enemies of the Lord to blaspheme,

---

[1] Isaiah i. 18.   [2] 1 John i. 9.

the child that is born unto thee shall surely die." God is not indifferent. He does not lightly pass by evil. He will mark His displeasure. The sin was forgiven at once. David puts it away, and God puts it away. The sinner is received back on his penitence to God's favor. But the effects of the sin remain. The penalty is still to be borne. The penalty was two-fold. (1) All David's prayer and fasting is unavailing to save the child's life. At last he resigns himself, "I shall go to him, but he shall not return to me." (2) And this was but the beginning of sorrows. That stroke fell at once. But it was followed by others. Other consequences of his crime remained to work out their terrible retribution. "The sword shall never depart from thine house." And it never did. David's earthly career was never afterwards what it had been before. The history of the remaining twenty years of his life was like a roll written within and without with lamentation and mourning and woe. Henceforward David had no respite from domestic affliction. His sin is repeated in the lives of his sons. He is repaid in his own coin. There follows the outrage on his daughter by incestuous Amnon; and the consequent murder of Amnon, his eldest son, by Absalom, Tamar's brother; this leads to the banishment of Absalom, his best beloved. Absalom conspires against his father, and drives him to an exile more grievous than that which he suffered in his youth when persecuted by Saul. Absalom is destroyed by Joab to David's unutterable grief, and against his express command. Joab, you remember, was in the king's secret, and had the whip hand of David; he was not going to be controlled. And then in the king's last years another son, Adonijah, plots against Solomon, whom David has marked out as his successor. "Whatsoever a man soweth, that shall he also reap." [1] All the subsequent history marks God's displeasure. Sooner or later there will be a day in which He will bring to light the hidden things of darkness,[2] and will vindicate His righteousness in the manifestation of His displeasure against wrongdoing, at which He may be thought to have winked. Be sure your sin will find you out.[3]

Now this is a marked illustration on a conspicuous scale of a general law. How full of instruction is the tale, in the way both of warning and of encouragement! We may well exclaim with an old English divine, "How can we presume of not sinning, or despair for sinning, when we find so great a saint thus fallen, thus risen?" [4] And surely not the least important lesson — both for warning and for encouragement — is found in the vindication of God's

[1] Galatians vi. 7.
[2] 1 Cor. iv. 5, Ps. l. 21.
[3] Numbers xxxii. 23.
[4] Bp. Jos. Hall, *Contemplations on the Old Testament*, bk. xv.

justice (along with the display of His mercy), in the lasting penalty of David's sin after he had been forgiven.

This marks a law of God's dealing with us all. In three ways we may mark and experience its working.

1. There are actual, external consequences of wrongdoing, — temporal consequences such as we thought about in an earlier discourse,[1] which, when regarded by themselves alone, may produce what St. Paul calls the sorrow of the world that worketh death — in despair and recklessness. The loss of health, or money, or position, these consequences survive, and have their effect both in ourselves and in others, long after sins have been bewailed in true repentance. Abstinence from the intoxicating draught does not replace a healthy step and clear complexion to the decayed and worn-out voluptuary; the bitterest regret does not restore the squandered talent or the wasted inheritance; the profoundest shame cannot give back lost innocence or forfeited honor. Coolness and suspicion on the part of others we may have to meet, and an inability in ourselves for service. Such things we must be ready to bear, and hope gradually to win back the forfeited position and trust by hard and patient struggle. Do not try to evade consequences. It is, I am sure, oftentimes

[1] Sermon II, p. 22.

false kindness to help others to evade them. It is better to help them to bear the consequences, and so work out their restoration. God's justice uses the consequences of sin to be its penalty, and then His mercy overrules the penalty to be its remedy.[1] So He leads us to see sin in its true light; not as the transgression of an arbitrary law, but as the violation of the abiding and eternal principle of right. Let us bravely and penitently say, "I will bear the indignation of the Lord, because I have sinned against Him."[2]

2. Besides these external consequences there are others of a more directly personal and spiritual kind. There are clinging habits of evil, haunting imaginations, the direct result of past indulgence, the difficulty we experience in prayer and our wandering thoughts, the dulled conscience and confusion of motives, a tongue-tied cowardice in rebuking evil on account of our own past wrongdoing. Such consequences remain "scourges in our sides and thorns in our eyes." We will not be discouraged nor fret and complain because of this. We have to begin where sin left off. We must take up the battle where we were defeated. Along with Christ, the

---

[1] St. Augustine distinguishes: "Ante remissionem esse illa supplicia peccatorum, post remissionem autem certamina exercitionesque justorum." — *De peccatorum meritis et remissione*, xi. 34.

[2] Micah vii. 9.

second Adam, we must fight our way from the
wilderness, among the wild beasts, to the Paradise
of innocence that we forfeited by following the
example of our first parents. In this light we see
that we may even *welcome* the recurrence of old
temptations, or of new ones which represent the
same general principle, as affording an opportunity
to reverse our former wrong choice, and so to
straighten out the tangle into which our nature has
fallen. It is only so that our moral restoration can be
gained. Sacraments, or the gift of the Spirit, cannot
work in us a *moral* change. That can only be the
result of our acts of choice. Our character *we*
ourselves must fashion, with the help of God, secured
by all the means that He has ordained. As with the
prodigal son, there are just so many steps to be re-
traced as we have wandered away from our Father's
house, only the journey is completed with the
assurance of the Father's support.

We will pray then,[1] Forgive, O Lord, the guilt,
heal the wound, blot out the stain, prevent the mis-
chief of my sin, renew in me whatever has been
decayed by the fraud and malice of the devil, or the
weakness of my own nature; and give me strength
to bear the consequences of my sin. Inflict what
penalty thou wilt, but cast me not away.

[1] Comp. Bp. Andrewes, *Devotions*, Order of Evening Prayer.

3. Lastly, behind and beneath these consequences — external and internal — there is our own remembrance of our sin, with shame and sorrow to think that we should have been guilty of such dishonesty or indulgence, such neglect or hatefulness, such ingratitude or rebelliousness. This will deepen as time goes on, because we learn more of the love and goodness against which the wrong has been committed. It may less and less disturb our peace, but the very assurance of forgiveness will kindle deeper penitence. This we may well believe will last on through life and into the other world. In the intermediate state between death and the last great day the soul, freed from the distractions of the world and from the deadening influence of the body, will see itself and God and all things as they truly are.[1] In deepening penitence shall be deepening purification, until in perfected penitence shall be found perfected purification. So we are told that St. Peter morning by morning wept as he heard the cock crow, and was reminded of his shameful denial of his Master. So St. Paul himself shows us in his letters that he kept in remembrance his former attitude as an enemy of the Lord Jesus, even though this was due to ignorance and unbelief.[2] He speaks of himself as the last of the apostles, not meet to be called an

[1] Martensen, *Christian Dogmatics*, V, § 276.
[2] Eph. iii. 8, 1 Tim. i. 13, 1 Cor. xv. 9, 10.

apostle, because he had persecuted the Church of God; as less than the least of all the consecrated ones; as the chief of sinners, once a blasphemer, a persecutor, and injurious. But he says, " By the grace of God I am what I am." Let this be our ambition, whatever may have been the past, that we may be made monuments of God's grace. The remembrance of former sin will not then be enfeebling, but will stimulate to greater earnestness and devotion now and for the future. "As it was your mind to go astray from God: so, being returned, seek Him ten times more." [1]

[1] Baruch iv. 28.

VII

THE GIFT OF THE SPIRIT FOR THE OFFICE AND WORK OF A PRIEST

VII

THE GIFT OF THE SPIRIT FOR THE OFFICE AND WORK OF A PRIEST

Then said Jesus to them again, Peace be unto you: as my Father hath sent me, even so send I you. And when he had said this, he breathed on them, and saith unto them, Receive ye the Holy Ghost: whose soever sins ye remit, they are remitted unto them; and whose soever sins ye retain, they are retained.[1]

John xx. 21–23.

I. TREMENDOUS words these are, — spoken (mark the occasion) by our Lord Jesus Christ to His apostles on the evening of Easter Day.[2] You will presently hear them repeated. Along with the laying-on of hands, the bishop will say to the candidate to be ordained, "Receive the Holy Ghost for the Office and Work of a Priest in the Church of God, now committed unto thee by the imposition of our hands. Whose sins thou dost forgive, they are forgiven; and

---

[1] The Greek should be noted: Εἰρήνη ὑμῖν. καθὼς ἀπέσταλκέ με ὁ πατήρ, κἀγὼ πέμπω ὑμᾶς . . . λάβετε πνεῦμα ἅγιον. ἄν τινων ἀφῆτε τὰς ἁμαρτίας, ἀφίενται αὐτοῖς · ἄν τινων κρατῆτε, κεκράτηνται.

[2] Others seem to have been present beside the apostles (Luke xxiv. 33). But the commission may well have been given to the apostles in the presence of the larger number of disciples. Or if the words were addressed to all, the Church would execute the commission through its officers.

whose sins thou dost retain, they are retained. And
be thou a faithful Dispenser of the Word of God, and
of his holy Sacraments; In the Name of the Father,
and of the Son, and of the Holy Ghost. Amen." The
Lord's own words are repeated now; for the office
of the ministry to which we set apart a man is the
same with that to which Christ ordained the apostles;
and the power by which it is to be executed is the
same. The apostles, of course, had their special
function as witnesses to Christ's life and teaching,
and more particularly to His resurrection; they were
to tell to others what they themselves had seen and
heard; and they were to be under Him founders of
the Church.[1] These were their peculiar functions;
but so far as the ministry of grace is concerned, the
preaching of the Word and the administration of the
Sacraments, they had no peculiar prerogative. It
was not because Peter or James or John, or the rest
of the apostles, were men of extraordinary ability
or of unusual personal gifts, that they were bidden
by the Lord to teach and baptize, to absolve, to feed
or rule His people. Such an idea would indeed show
"man-worship" of the worst kind, as if they acted
by their own power; whereas in all they did they
were representatives of the Lord who commissioned
them.[2] "As the Father hath sent me [He said], so

[1] Acts i. 8, 21, 22, x. 41, Eph. ii. 20, Rev. xxi. 14.
[2] 1 Cor. iv. 1, Gal. iv. 14, 2 Cor. v. 20.

send I you." "Receive the Holy Spirit" for your
work. This may suffice to justify the application of
Christ's words in our form of ordination.[1]

II. What, then, we ask, is the meaning of our
Lord's words that we thus use? "Receive the Holy
Ghost; whose soever sins ye remit, they are remitted unto them; and whose soever sins ye retain,
they are retained." About the second clause I would
ask you to note three things.

1. First, the words state the general commission
given to the Church to proclaim Forgiveness of sins
on the condition of Repentance.[2] By Forgiveness
is meant (as I explained in the Lenten sermons)[3] a
great deal more than the mere letting off of the punishment of wrongdoing; it is restoration as well as

---

[1] It is sometimes urged that since the apostles were endowed
with the power of working miracles, they might also be expected
to exercise supernatural powers of a spiritual kind. But (1) the
power of working miracles was not confined to the apostles, nor
was it an exclusively ministerial prerogative; it belonged to early
Christians as disciples rather than apostles. ("These signs shall
follow them that believe," Mark xvi. 17.) (2) Being granted for
the purpose of introducing the new religion into the world and
giving to it divine sanction, miracles were (for the most part) withdrawn when they had served this purpose. "The duration of any
gift depends upon the need which it supplies." — Newman's
sermon on "The Christian Ministry," in vol. II of his *Parochial
Sermons*.

[2] Luke xxiv. 47, Acts v. 31.

[3] Sermon I, p. 12.

acquittal, release and not only pardon, deliverance from the power as well as from the guilt of sin. This is the promise of the risen Lord; it is the consequence of His victorious sacrifice. Man, in the person of the incarnate Son of God, has conquered; men and women can conquer after His example and by His aid. Forgiveness and remission of sins is promised to all who truly desire it, on the condition of their true repentance. Man must desire to be freed, if his chains are to be loosed; he must draw near to God, if he is to find God drawing near to him; he must open his heart, if God is to bestow His gifts.

The gift of pardon is for the penitent and well-disposed. They that are whole have no need of the physician, but they that are sick. Christ came not to call the righteous, but sinners to repentance. The hungry, who are conscious of their need, He ever fills with good things: the rich, and self-satisfied, He sends empty away.[1] In insisting upon the terms for forgiveness, and proclaiming forgiveness to those who truly repent, the Church remits the sins of some and retains the sins of others. God "hath given power and commandment to His Ministers, to declare and pronounce to His people, being penitent, the Absolution and Remission of their sins."

2. This forgiveness and reconciliation with God (which involves the power of a new life as well as

---

[1] Mark ii. 17, Luke i. 53.

pardon for the past) is specially pledged and sealed to us in the Sacraments which Christ ordained — Baptism and the Supper of the Lord, the sacred Washing and the sacred Meal. In Baptism our inner nature is cleansed by the Spirit of God, as our body is washed with water; its inward gift is a death unto sin and a new birth unto righteousness. In Holy Communion, as we show our Lord's death and glory in His victory, the virtue and benefits of His sacrifice are continually applied to us. We receive the Body which was broken, and the Blood which was shed for the remission of sins.[1]

3. The Church, acting through its appointed Ministry, the body through its proper organs, is entrusted with the administration of these life-giving Sacraments, and is to admit to or exclude from them according as she recognizes the fitness or the unfitness of applicants. This judgment may be exercised in a broad and general way.

(a) The Church lays down and constantly proclaims the conditions on which persons may be admitted to Baptism and to Holy Communion. The Catechism tells what is required of persons to be baptized: Repentance, whereby they forsake sin; and Faith, whereby they steadfastly lay hold of the promises of God. The candidate for Baptism solemnly promises to renounce all evil, to believe God's

---

[1] 1 Cor. xi. 23–26, Matt. xxvi. 28.

revelation, to obey His will. Of those who come to the Lord's Supper are required repentance, faith, and charity. "Ye who do truly and earnestly repent you of your sins, and are in love and charity with your neighbors, and intend to lead a new life, following the commandments of God, and walking from henceforth in His holy ways; Draw near with faith, and take this holy Sacrament to your comfort."

(b) When these conditions are made known, the Church very largely throws persons upon the judgment of their own conscience as to their correspondence with the terms laid down.[1]

(c) In cases of obvious and grave violations of Christian rules she suspends persons from her privileges, and forbids them to approach the holy Table, until by God's mercy they are brought to a better mind, and then on satisfactory evidence of their true repentance they may be restored to Communion. Thus, in the exercise of discipline, sins are retained and remitted, by exclusion from or admission to the Sacraments and means of grace.

(d) The wide commission to the Church is not to be narrowed as if it primarily referred to a private absolution; nevertheless, it distinctly covers the absolution which an individual priest may give to a person seeking special help. Each particular priest

---

[1] This is well put in Wm. Allen Whitworth's *The Real Presence with other Essays*, a valuable little book.

among the people committed to his care, and subject to appeal to the higher authority of the chief pastor, is to enforce the rules laid down by the Church, to admit persons to Baptism or Holy Communion in accordance therewith; in cases where persons are doubtful and burdened in conscience it is his duty to help them to resolve their doubts, get rid of their scruples, and ease their consciences. He will pray for and with such a person; he will invoke upon him God's mercy and blessing; acting as an impartial judge, in the name of God and on behalf of the Church, he will accept the man's penitence, and will bring home to him the assurance of God's pardon; and thus enable him to come to Communion with a quiet conscience. This is a form of absolution. Thus the commission given to the apostles with regard to men in general covers and includes the particular priest's dealing with the individual penitent.

When we seize these points, we see that, great and tremendous as our Lord's words are, there is nothing unreasonable about them or their application. "Whose soever sins ye remit, they are remitted unto them; and whose soever sins ye retain, they are retained." All, of course, is done in Christ's name, by His authority. All is subject to His ratification, is done under appeal to Him, the supreme Judge, who alone can read the secrets of men's hearts.

III. This leads naturally to the words on which I desire more particularly to lay stress. "Who is sufficient for these things?" we may well ask. "Receive the Holy Ghost for the office and work of a priest in the Church of God," is the Church's answer, echoing the words of our Lord. Let us be clear about the meaning of this gift.

1. It is no claim to confer *magical power*, as uninstructed persons sometimes imagine, as if the Spirit of God were to enable a man to perform conjuring tricks; as if by his mere word or the touch of his hand a spiritual effect were produced; as if the water in Baptism cleansed the heart, or the bread and wine in Holy Communion fed the soul. In sacraments there is an outward visible sign, and an inward spiritual grace. Each is true and real in its own order, — the outward sign for our physical nature, the inward grace for our spiritual being. What we look for from the gift of the Spirit of God to His ministers is, in part, that when they perform according to His institution the outward ceremony, the inward grace, symbolized by the sign, may accompany their act,[1] the benefit, of course, being only for recipients who approach the ministration with right dispositions.

[1] "Whether we preach, pray, baptize, communicate, condemn, give absolution, or whatsoever, as disposers of God's mysteries, our words, judgments, acts, and deeds are not ours but the Holy Ghost's." — Hooker, *Eccles. Pol.*, V, lxxvii, 8.

2. The words "Receive the Holy Ghost" tell of no mere investing with *external authority*. For this, the expression would be indeed extravagant and ill chosen.

3. The words point to a gift of spiritual ability: receive the Holy Spirit, or a special manifestation of His presence,[1] to enable you to discharge this ministry to the souls of men.

Mark the accompanying action of our Lord. He breathed on His disciples as He said these words. This was a sort of sacrament, an outward visible sign of an inward spiritual gift. He, the risen Lord, perfected through suffering, imparts to His disciples the life that was in Himself, the Holy Spirit as dwelling in Himself. By the Spirit of God His human nature had been fashioned; in the power of the Spirit He had accomplished His ministry; through the eternal Spirit He had offered Himself without spot to God.[2] The apostles are to be enabled to carry on His work by sharing His Spirit. This is what we mean now when we say, "Receive the Holy Ghost for the office and work of a priest in the Church of God." The priest is to do Christ's work, in

[1] πνεῦμα ἅγιον without the article.

[2] Luke i. 35, iv. 1, 14, Heb. ix. 14. Comp. Newman in the sermon quoted above (p. 303), "Our Lord was solemnly anointed with the Holy Ghost, as an initiation into His priestly office. He was manifested as receiving, that He might be believed on as giving," etc.

Christ's name, with Christ's authority, after Christ's fashion, by the aid of Christ's Spirit.   Let me give three or four illustrations of what I mean.

(a) The priest is to deal with sinners and with sin as Christ would, as He did.   He must hate the sin, while he pities the sinner; abhor uncleanness, false-hood, cruelty, while he is full of compassion for those who have become entangled in the lusts of the flesh, the deceits of the world, or the snares of the devil. "Go thy way," said our Lord to the woman taken in adultery; "from henceforth sin no more." [1]   By the aid of the Spirit of Christ the priest must learn more and more to see all — persons and things, sinners and sin — with the eyes of Christ, in the light of God.   Thus will he be saved at once from harshness towards others, and from himself being contaminated by the evil with which he must come in contact as he seeks to deliver others from its influence.   Some he will save with fear, pulling them out of the fire, hating even the garment spotted with the flesh.[2]

(b) By sharing Christ's Spirit he will gain some-thing of Christ's discrimination, the "discerning of spirits," learning to distinguish between the mere action, good or bad, and the motive which prompts it and gives it color, the character out of which it springs.   So will he learn to judge righteous judgment.

[1] John viii. 11.   [2] Jude 22.

(c) In another way the priest guided by Christ's Spirit will act with the consideration and gentleness of Christ. He taught the people as they were able to receive His word, speaking to the multitude in parables, while deeper truths He reserved for the inner circle of His chosen disciples. So must we lead people on gently, taking care not to repel or over-drive, adapting ourselves and our teaching to the actual men and women with whom we have to do, considering their mental and spiritual capacities.

(d) Once more. You will hear the candidate promise to be diligent to make himself a wholesome example and pattern to the people committed to his charge. This is how Christ our Lord taught. In His own conduct He exemplified the character He would impress upon His disciples. If He taught Blessed, or Happy, are the poor in spirit, the meek, the merciful, and so forth, He illustrated in His own life the beauty and joy of the virtues which He praised. So ought we priests to live the faith, to be pattern-believers in word and conduct (the out-ward expressions of our religion), in love and faith (its inward principles), in purity (its consecrating grace).[1] We ought to give an example of humility and obedience, of unworldliness and patience, of courage and honor. So shall we win people by our lives even more than by our words. And this is

[1] 1 Tim. iv. 12.

made possible by the gift of Christ's Spirit, through whom we gain His mind and reproduce His character, and so share His influence.

Here, before concluding, I must give two cautions, or make two explanations.

1. It is true that the unworthiness of evil ministers hinders not the effect of the sacraments.[1] The proclamation of God's Word, though it be by one who follows not his own teaching, may win to God and His service those who hear it. The efficacy of the sacred Washing is not hindered because it is administered by one who is untrue to the obligations and the privileges of his own Baptism. The Eucharist, though the celebrating priest partake of it to his own condemnation, avails to the nourishing and refreshing of those who draw near with right dispositions. All this is so, because the priest is acting not in his own name, but as the representative on earth of the heavenly Priest, who acts through His ministers, or even in spite of their personal unworthiness, and blesses His own ordinances to those who rightly approach them.[2]

But anything of this kind is, we recognize, abnormal. It is not what Christ intended, this miserable divorce between the person and the office. Christ means His ministers to be not merely instru-

---

[1] Article XXVI.
[2] Luke x. 16, 1 Cor. iii. 5–7; comp. Matt. xxiii. 2, 3.

ments, but agents, with whom He works by the gift
of His Spirit. If we do not ask how much is *lost* by
the failure of the man to correspond with his office —
lost through his neglect and inconsistency and scandal — we can see what is *gained* by the realization
(however imperfect) of the ideal, when the priest's
life is in accordance with the truth he teaches, and
his character is seen to be transformed by the grace
he ministers. Here is the presence of the Spirit for
the office and work of a priest.

> In word and deed, by heart and tongue,
> With all our powers Thy praise be sung.
> Inflame with perfect love each sense,
> That others' souls may kindle thence.

2. Another word of explanation. *All* need God's
aid, and must seek Christ's Spirit, for their life and
work whatever it may be — in the performance of
any duties, domestic, social, civic, or professional.
But a *special* gift of Christ's Spirit we ask for the
special work of the ministry in dealing with souls,
with men's inner life of heart and conscience. It is
with no disparagement of other callings, in no denial
of their sacredness, that the Church says, "Receive
the Holy Ghost for the office and work of a priest in
the Church of God," and prays in the *Veni Creator* for
the Spirit's special gifts for the man to be ordained.

8

Pray then for him who is to be entrusted with this responsible office, that he may indeed receive the Holy Spirit for the office and work of a priest in the Church of God. And that he may not only receive the gift now, but that he may continually stir up this gift.[1] As with Baptism and Confirmation, the gift of the Spirit for the ministry is not bestowed once for all at the ministration of the sacrament; rather there is set up a new relationship between the man and God, a gift is pledged to the man from that time forward; it is a boundless gift placed at our disposal on which we are continually to draw.

Pray that Christ's Spirit may enable him to fulfil the solemn promises you will hear him make; that Christ's Spirit may fit him to execute the ministry of God's Word and Sacraments committed to him.

Pray that Christ's Spirit may bind him in fellowship of life with Christ, that so he may carry on Christ's work for the benefit of Christ's people.

[1] 2 Timothy, i. 6.

NOTE ON THE
ANOINTING OF THE SICK

NOTE ON THE ANOINTING OF THE SICK

(Page 79)

The matter of Anointing the Sick has been a good deal discussed of late (especially in connection with the claims of Christian Science, Faith Healing, etc.), and a proposal has been made for its authoritative reintroduction among ourselves. It may then be worth while to note the following points for consideration:

1. In the passage from St. James's Epistle (v. 14–16), the solemn impetration of God's help, the prayer of the presbyters, is clearly the *chief* thing.

2. This was distinctly for *bodily* healing (corresponding with the promise of our Lord in Mark xvi. 18), the forgiveness of sins being separately treated.

3. There is no reason to suppose that the oil was intended to have a *sacramental* effect. It might (as suggested in the sermon) stand for the application of a *natural* remedy; or, more probably, because often used as a natural remedy, be a *symbol* (appealing to the imagination) of the healing which was sought by prayer.

A sacrament, as an outward and visible sign (applied to the body) of an inward and spiritual grace (for the soul) it cannot be, if its object is bodily healing. According to the Roman Catholic use of unction of the sick as a spiritual preparation for death, it may rightly be called a sacrament; but then this use is altogether lacking in authority or warrant from our Lord or His apostles.

It was not until the end of the 8th or the 9th century that the remission of sins was definitely connected with the unction.

4. In harmony with what is said above is the lack of evidence as to the continuous practice in the early Church of anointing the sick as a religious rite.

The *symbolic* use of the oil was no *binding precept* of the apostle; he recommended its use along with prayer as a practice which at the time was customary and would be helpful (as our Lord had done, Mark vi. 13). For a time Christians anointed themselves or others with oil that had or had not been previously blessed. It was not until the 10th century that the administration of unction was reserved to the priest, and by this time the idea of a *spiritual* gift had come to be associated with it.

5. In any revival of the custom that might be authorized it would be most desirable to keep entirely separate the thought of the forgiveness of sins from the anointing, which should be distinctly with a view to bodily healing, as an accompaniment of prayer.

For this reason the form provided for its administration ("if the sick person desire it"), in the Prayer-book of 1549, would be unsuitable, since this refers to spiritual benefits: "As with this oil thy body outwardly is anointed, so our heavenly Father, Almighty God, grant of his infinite goodness that thy soul inwardly may be anointed with the Holy Ghost, who is the Spirit of all strength, comfort, relief, and gladness." This point is strongly urged by the Rev. F. W. Puller in his exhaustive discussion of the whole subject, *The Anointing of the Sick in Scripture and Tradition* (S. P. C. K. 1904). See also J. B. Mayor, *The Epistle of St. James*, pp. 165–167, 227, 228.

The University Press, Cambridge, U. S. A.